Lead Arsenate. I. Composition of Lead Arsenates Found on the Market ; II. "Home-made" Lead Arsenate and the Chemicals Entering Into Its Manufacture ; III. Action of Lead Arsenate on Foliage

Issued April 6, 1910.

U. S. DEPARTMENT OF AGRICULTURE,

BUREAU OF CHEMISTRY—BULLETIN No. 131.

H. W. WILEY, Chief of Bureau.

LEAD ARSENATE.

I. Composition of lead arsenates found on the market.
II. "Home-made" lead arsenate and the chemicals entering into its manufacture.
III. Action of lead arsenate on foliage.

BY

J. K. HAYWOOD,

Chief, Miscellaneous Division,

AND

C. C. McDONNELL,

Chief, Insecticide and Fungicide Laboratory, Miscellaneous Division.

IN COOPERATION WITH THE BUREAU OF ENTOMOLOGY.

WASHINGTON:
GOVERNMENT PRINTING OFFICE.
1910.

LETTER OF TRANSMITTAL

U S DEPARTMENT OF AGRICULTURE,
BUREAU OF CHEMISTRY,
Washington, D C , October 16, 1909

SIR I have the honor to submit for your approval a report on the composition of commercial and "home-made" lead arsenates, together with the results of two years' experimental work on the action of this insecticide on foliage, especially that of the peach tree. The problems and conditions discussed are of vital interest to all orchardists and farmers, and I recommend the publication of the report as Bulletin 131 of the Bureau of Chemistry. The work was performed in the insecticide and fungicide laboratory of the Miscellaneous Division of this Bureau, with the cooperation of the Bureau of Entomology

Respectfully,

H. W. WILEY,
Chief of Bureau.

Hon JAMES WILSON,
Secretary of Agriculture.

2

CONTENTS

ILLUSTRATIONS.

PLATES.

TEXT FIGURE.

LEAD ARSENATE.

INTRODUCTION.

It is only in more recent years that lead arsenate has been used as an insecticide for spraying purposes. Its use was first suggested by Mr. F. C. Moulton in 1892, while acting as chemist for the gypsy moth commission of Massachusetts, after having made a study of numerous materials to be used as insecticides for the extermination of the gypsy moth. It was found that Paris green could not be used successfully for this purpose, principally because it could not be applied in sufficient quantity to kill the caterpillars without seriously injuring the foliage. While lead arsenate was not found entirely satisfactory in destroying this pest, it possessed several advantages over Paris green, and this has resulted in its replacing the latter material for spraying purposes to a very large extent, in fact, almost entirely in some of the Rocky Mountain and Pacific Coast States. Some of these advantages are: (1) It is not so injurious to foliage when applied thereto, on account of its being less soluble in water. (2) When sprayed upon leaves it forms a thin film, which is quite adhesive and is not so easily washed off by rains. (3) It remains in suspension much better, thereby requiring less effort to keep the mixture agitated, and thus insuring a more uniform application. (4) Being white, it forms a visible coating and is easily distinguished when it has been applied.

The initial cost of this material is slightly greater than that of Paris green, owing to the fact that it contains a smaller percentage of arsenic than the latter, and therefore more of it must be used to produce the same effect. Because of its greater adhesive qualities, however, it remains on the foliage better, requiring less frequent application, and thus in the end lead arsenate is no more expensive than Paris green, in fact, it may be even cheaper, as the greatest expense in spraying is the cost of applying the material to the trees.

The use of lead arsenate has increased very rapidly during the last few years, as is shown by the fact that less than ten years ago no one was manufacturing it to any large extent, while at the present time there are at least eighteen manufacturing chemists in the United States making it in greater or less quantities, and a number of other firms are preparing to do so. An attempt was made to determine the total amount sold in the United States for the years 1907 and 1908 by writing to the various manufacturers for figures showing their sales.

Many of these very cheerfully gave the information asked for, but several refused, and a few others did not have the data available. Judging from the information which has been obtained, the total amount sold in 1908 was approximately 2,500 tons, the value of which was more than half a million dollars. In addition, a great quantity of the home-made material has been used, but this quantity can not be estimated.

It was on account of the great importance which lead arsenate is assuming for spraying purposes and in view of certain variable results which have been reported, that this study was begun by the Bureau of Chemistry two years ago, principally for the purpose of determining, if possible, the conditions which cause it to be injurious to foliage in some cases. The experiments have been conducted for two successive years, as it was considered impossible to arrive at any trustworthy conclusions in a shorter period. At the same time a study of the composition of the lead arsenates found on the market and also that of "home-made" lead arsenate was made, including analyses of such of the chemicals entering into its manufacture as could be procured from druggists and other sources.

This work, therefore, has been divided into three parts, as follows: I. Composition of lead arsenates found on the market. II. "Home-made" lead arsenate, and the chemicals entering into its manufacture. III. Action of lead arsenate on foliage.

The work has been carried out in cooperation with the Bureau of Entomology, Mr. A. L. Quaintance, in charge of deciduous-fruit insect investigations, having furnished the larger number of the samples herein reported and cooperated in the carrying out of the spraying experiments outlined in the third section.

I. COMPOSITION OF LEAD ARSENATES FOUND ON THE MARKET.

SCOPE OF THE INVESTIGATION.

The object of this investigation was to determine by chemical analysis the quality or grade of the leading lead arsenates as found on the open market and supplied to the trade. To this end samples were obtained at many points in different sections of the United States by various collectors, and, while the products of a few manufacturers are not represented, all of the leading brands, representing about 98 per cent of the total output, are included in the list. In a number of instances several samples of the same brand, purchased at different times and places, have been analyzed in order to determine whether the output of the same firm is of uniform composition. As the purpose of the investigation was to show the general condition of the trade during 1907–8, more particularly as a preliminary to other studies, the names of the manufacturers are not given, but all of the samples from one firm are designated by the same letter, that

METHODS OF ANALYSIS.

The samples were analyzed according to the provisional methods of the Association of Official Agricultural Chemists [a], as follows·

PREPARATION OF SAMPLE

In case the sample is in the form of a paste, as it usually is, dry the whole of it to constant weight at the temperature of boiling water and calculate the results as total moisture Grind the dry sample (which will gain a small amount of moisture by so doing) to a fine powder and determine the various constituents as follows

MOISTURE

Weigh 2 grams of the sample and heat in a water bath for eight hours or in a hot air bath at 110° C for from five to six hours, or till constant weight is obtained

TOTAL LEAD OXID

Dissolve 2 grams of the sample in about 80 cc of water and 15 cc of concentrated nitric acid on the steam bath, transfer the solution to a 250 cc flask, and make up to the mark To 50 cc of the solution add 3 cc of concentrated sulphuric acid, evaporate on the steam bath to a sirupy consistency, and then on the hot plate till white fumes appear and all nitric acid has been given off Add 50 cc of water and 100 cc of 95 per cent alcohol Let stand for several hours and filter off supernatant liquid, wash about ten times with acidified alcohol (water 100 parts, 95 per cent alcohol 200 parts, and concentrated sulphuric acid 3 parts), and then with 95 per cent alcohol till free of sulphuric acid Dry, remove as much as possible of the precipitate from the paper into a weighed crucible, and ignite at low red heat Burn the paper in a separate porcelain crucible and treat the residue first with a little nitric acid, which is afterwards evaporated off, and then with a drop or two of dilute sulphuric acid Ignite, weigh, and add this weight to the weight of the precipitate previously removed from the paper for amount of the lead sulphate If preferred, the lead sulphate may be filtered and weighed in a porcelain Gooch crucible

TOTAL ARSENIC OXID (MODIFIED GOOCH AND BROWNING METHOD [b])

Transfer 100 cc of the nitric acid solution of the sample, prepared as in the above determination of lead, to a porcelain dish, add 6 cc of concentrated sulphuric acid, evaporate to a sirupy consistency on water bath and then on hot plate to the appearance of white fumes of sulphuric acid Wash into a 100 cc flask with water, make up to mark, filter through dry filter, and use a 50 cc aliquot for further work Transfer this to an Erlenmeyer flask of 400 cc capacity, add 4 cc of concentrated sulphuric acid and 1 gram of potassium iodid, dilute to about 100 cc and boil until the volume is reduced to about 40 cc Cool the solution under running water, dilute to about 300 cc, and exactly use up the iodin set free and still remaining in solution with a few drops of approximately tenth-normal sodium thiosulphate Wash the mixture into a large beaker, make alkaline with sodium carbonate and slightly acidify with dilute sulphuric acid, then make alkaline again with an excess of sodium bicarbonate Titrate the solution with a twentieth-normal iodin solution to the appearance of a blue color, using starch as indicator

WATER-SOLUBLE LEAD OXID

Place 2 grams of the sample in a flask with 2,000 cc of carbon-dioxid-free water and let stand ten days, shaking eight times a day Filter through a dry filter (being sure a clear filtrate is obtained) and use aliquots of this for determining soluble lead and arsenic oxids and soluble solids, determine lead as described above for total lead,

---

[a] U S Dept Agr , Bureau of Chemistry Bul 107, Revised, p 239
[b] Amer. J. Sci., 1890, *40*. 66

using the same relative proportions of sulphuric acid, water, and alcohol, but keeping the volume as small as possible

WATER-SOLUBLE ARSENIC OXID

For this determination use 200 to 400 cc of the water extract obtained under the determination of soluble lead oxid Add 0 5 cc of sulphuric acid and evaporate it to a sirupy consistency, then heat on a hot plate to appearance of white fumes Add a very small amount of water and filter off lead through the very smallest filter paper, using as little wash water as possible Place this filtrate in an Erlenmeyer flask, and determine arsenic as described under total arsenic oxid, using the same amount of reagents and the same dilutions

SOLUBLE SOLIDS OR IMPURITIES

Evaporate 200 cc of the water extract obtained above to dryness in a weighed platinum dish, dry to constant weight at the temperature of the boiling water bath, and weigh The soluble solids so obtained represent principally any sodium acetate or sodium nitrate present, with a very small quantity perhaps of lead acetate or nitrate and some soluble arsenic, probably in the form of lead arsenate, or sodium arsenate

These methods were not followed exactly in all cases, owing to peculiarities of some of the samples Those which were moist and in the form of a paste were heated at about 85° C. till dry enough to powder, and the loss noted The analysis was then carried out on this dried sample and the results calculated to the material in its original condition. The moisture on the dried sample was calculated to the original material and added to the loss obtained on the first drying for "total moisture"

Insoluble matter was that remaining from the treatment with nitric acid and was removed by filtration, washed, ignited, and weighed.

In case calcium is present in the sample, it may be separated from the lead by treating the precipitated sulphates with water (acidified with sulphuric acid) to which no alcohol has been added and filtering, or by the following method, which is the one used in this work:

Precipitate the lead from a solution slightly acidified with nitric acid, with hydrogen sulphid in the cold, filter off the precipitate containing the lead sulphid, wash, dissolve in moderately strong hot nitric acid, treat this solution with 4 or 5 cc of concentrated sulphuric acid, carry down in a porcelain dish to expel nitric acid, treat with water and alcohol mixture, and proceed as before Calcium is determined in the filtrate from the lead sulphid (after removing any arsenic remaining therein by hydrogen sulphid) by precipitating with ammonia and ammonium oxalate in the regular way

In case the material was lead arsenite or contained this substance, it was determined as follows

Boil 2 grams of the sample with 50 cc of dilute (1 to 5) sulphuric acid for about one hour, cool, make up to mark, filter through dry filter, and to 50 cc of the filtrate add sodium bicarbonate in considerable excess and titrate with standard iodin solution, using starch as indicator The arsenic equivalent of the iodin solution used is calculated as arsenious oxid (As_2O_3)

Tests were made on the water soluble impurities for acetates and nitrates This would indicate which lead salt had been used in the manufacture of the sample.

RESULTS OF ANALYSES.

Table I.—*Composition of commercial lead arsenates.*
ANALYSIS OF ORIGINAL SAMPLE.

Serial number and letter indicating firm.	Moisture.	Acid insoluble.	Total lead oxid (PbO).	Total arsenic oxid (As$_2$O$_5$).	Water-soluble impurities.	Water-soluble lead oxid (PbO).	Water-soluble arsenic oxid (As$_2$O$_5$).	Soluble impurities contain—
A:	*Per cent.*	*Per cent.*	*Per cent.*	*Per cent.*	*Per cent.*	*Per cent.*	*Per cent.*	
4535	61.84	0.03	23.06	12.62	2.03	0.15	0.31	Nitrates.
4629	44.69	.05	35.45	17.97	.55	.06	.38	Do.
4656	59.65	.04	25.27	13.66	.75	.09	.22	Do.
5084	47.91	.03	32.50	17.13	.80	.18	.33	Do.
5086	40.63	.14	42.23	14.49	1.34	.75	.50	Acetates.
5087	52.02	.03	30.06	15.64	.65	.09	.25	Nitrates.
5088	48.21	.04	32.11	16.99	.99	.16	.33	Do.
5089	45.60	.02	35.53	16.93	.32	.29	.43	Do.
5090	42.75	.06	36.07	17.55	1.42	.25	.37	Do.
5853	.41	.05	66.75	28.91	.66	1.06	1.06	Acetates.
5854	48.05	.04	32.75	16.86	1.51	.31	.32	Nitrates.
6451	41.36	....	37.79	17.38	.76	.48	.82	Acetates.
B:								
6456	42.61	....	39.49	14.44	1.06	.32	.41	Do.
C:								
a 5341	44.70	....	41.46	12.16	.08	.28	.11	Do.
D:								
4633	36.89	.28	39.75	17.76	4.51	.16	.50	Do.
b 4651	46.38	.03	35.03	14.65	3.71	.17	.22	Do.
b 4652	37.76	.11	40.66	17.23	3.20	.18	.30	Do.
5085	37.61	.08	40.92	17.76	1.27	.21	.36	Do.
5091	31.54	.00	48.09	15.69	2.18	.22	.22	Do.
5961	41.18	.05	35.48	18.81	4.33	.55	.20	Nitrates.
6452	21.41	....	46.80	22.11	5.68	.67	.06	Do.
E:								
c 4720	45.60	3.42	26.97	12.08	7.54	1.19	2.42	Acetates.
F:								
4291	40.89	....	36.46	19.60	1.04	.37	.33	
b 4301	48.29	.04	33.89	15.46	2.23	.29	.33	Do.
G:								
4533	28.39	.04	49.67	20.49	2.03	.49	1.01	Do.
5611	37.89	....	43.88	14.87	.77	.10	.13	Do.
5855	1.89	.05	64.54	28.06	3.80	1.04	1.08	Do.
5856	45.60	.03	37.93	14.33	.64	.30	.41	Do.
6454	34.24	....	45.64	16.90	.75	.58	.90	Do.
H:								
4534	.57	.09	72.57	24.01	1.14	.47	.51	Do.
6453	48.34	....	36.88	11.98	1.04	.44	.04	Do.
I:								
4296	43.08	....	38.81	15.22	2.32	.22	.23	Nitrates.
4631	45.84	.03	35.25	16.76	1.34	.11	.24	Acetates.
4632	45.12	.29	35.82	16.70	.44	.12	.26	Do.
b 4648	45.20	.04	36.58	16.24	.68	.19	.30	Do.
4657	40.38	.11	40.04	17.83	.65	.36	.32	Do.
4721	.50	.03	67.14	28.87	2.01	.21	.44	Do.
4830	46.34	.07	34.44	16.56	.93	.13	.26	Do.
5852	.67	.67	65.24	26.42	1.39	.60	.58	Nitrates.
5959	47.56	.03	35.06	15.98	.74	.35	.39	Do.
4657	41.03	....	38.46	16.24	1.45	.44	.71	Do.
J:								
d 4644	2.00	.05	51.35	43.81	2.27	.44	5.45	Acetates.
K:								
6455	35.75	....	44.64	16.43	.67	.40	.87	Do.
L:								
e 4532	35.43	.06	44.73	18.04	.88	.63	2.12	Do.
f 6458	41.40	....	45.62	6.03	3.35	1.61	.02	....
M:								
4624	.76	.11	60.06	28.52	5.40	.38	.30	Nitrates.
N:								
4571	61.03	.23	23.31	12.89	2.03	.19	.21	Do.
4630	22.18	.09	50.55	25.15	.83	.29	.80	Acetates.
O:								
4870	38.81	.21	37.98	20.91	.45	.15	.45	Nitrates.
5960	43.26	.03	36.02	19.36	.40	.42	.53	Do.

a Sample had distinct odor of ammonia; on determination gave 0.14 per cent on original sample.
b Sample had decided acid reaction; strong odor of acetic acid.
c Contained 2.48 per cent of CaO, 1.75 per cent of CO$_2$; calculated to moisture-free basis, 4.56 per cent of CaO, 3.22 per cent of CO$_2$.
d Mostly lead arsenite. Total arsenic reported as As$_2$O$_3$, 43.81 per cent; of this, 3.37 per cent (⊂3.91 per cent As$_2$O$_5$) is present as arsenate; soluble arsenic reported as As$_2$O$_3$.
e Sample labeled "lead arsenite;" a mixture of lead arsenite and lead arsenate. Arsenic as arsenite 6.52 per cent of As$_2$O$_3$ (⊂7.57 per cent of As$_2$O$_5$); as arsenate 10.47 per cent of As$_2$O$_5$. Calculated to moisture-free basis As$_2$O$_3$=10.01 per cent; As$_2$O$_5$=16.31 per cent. Water-soluble arsenic reported as As$_2$O$_3$.
f Contains an excess of lead as carbonate.

TABLE I.—*Composition of commercial lead arsenates*—Continued.

CALCULATED TO MOISTURE-FREE BASIS.

Serial number and letter indicating firm.	Acid insoluble.	Total lead oxid (PbO).	Total arsenic oxid (As_2O_5).	Water-soluble impurities.	Water-soluble lead oxid (PbO).	Water-soluble arsenic oxid (As_2O_5).
A:	*Per cent.*	*Per cent.*	*Per cent.*	*Per cent.*	*Per cent.*	*Per cent.*
4535	0.08	60.43	33.07	5.32	0.39	0.81
4629	.09	64.09	32.49	.99	.11	.69
4656	.10	62.63	33.85	1.86	.22	.55
5084	.06	62.39	32.89	1.54	.35	.63
5086	.24	71.13	24.41	2.26	1.26	.84
5087	.07	62.65	32.60	1.35	.19	.52
5088	.68	62.00	32.81	1.91	.31	.64
5089	.03	65.31	31.12	.59	.53	.79
5090	.11	63.00	30.66	2.48	44	.65
5853	.05	67.03	29.03	.67	1.06	1.06
5854	.08	63.04	32.45	2.91	.60	.60
6451	....	64.44	29.64	1.30	.82	1.40
B:						
6456	....	68.80	25.16	1.85	.56	.71
C:						
5341	....	74.97	21.99	.14	.51	.20
D:						
4633	.44	62.09	28.14	7.15	.25	.79
4651	.06	65.33	27.32	6.91	.32	.41
4652	.18	65.33	27.68	5.14	.29	.48
5085	.13	65.59	28.47	2.04	.34	.58
5091	.09	70.25	22.92	3.18	.32	.32
5961	.09	60.32	31.98	7.36	.94	.34
6452	....	59.54	28.13	7.22	.85	.08
E:						
4720	6.29	49.58	22.21	13.86	2.19	4.45
F:						
4291	....	61.68	33.16	1.76	.63	.56
4301	....	65.54	29.90	4.31	.56	.64
G:						
4533	.06	69.36	28.61	2.83	.68	1.41
5611	....	70.65	23.94	1.24	.16	.21
5855	.05	65.78	28.60	3.87	1.06	1.10
5856	.06	69.72	26.34	1.18	.55	.77
6454	....	69.40	25.69	1.14	.88	1.37
H:						
4534	.09	72.99	24.15	1.15	.47	.51
6453	....	71.39	23.19	2.01	.85	.08
I:						
4296	....	68.18	26.74	4.08	.40	.40
4631	.06	65.08	30.95	2.47	.20	.44
4632	.53	65.27	30.43	.80	.22	.47
4648	.07	66.75	29.64	1.24	.35	.55
4657	.18	67.16	29.91	1.09	.60	.54
4721	.03	67.54	29.04	2.02	.21	.44
4830	.13	64.18	30.86	1.73	.24	.48
5852	.67	65.68	26.60	1.40	.60	.58
5959	.06	66.86	30.47	1.41	.67	.74
4657	....	65.20	27.54	2.47	.75	1.20
J:						
4644	.05	52.40	44.70	2.32	.45	5.56
K:						
6455	....	69.48	25.57	1.04	.62	1.35
L:						
4532	.09	69.27	27.94	1.36	.98	3.28
6455	....	77.93	10.30	5.72	2.75	.03
M:						
4624	.11	60.52	28.74	5.44	.38	.30
N:						
4571	.59	59.82	33.08	5.21	.50	.54
4630	.12	64.96	32.32	1.07	.37	1.08
O:						
4870	.34	62.07	34.17	.74	.24	.74
5960	.05	63.48	34.12	.70	.74	.93

DISCUSSION.

Some of the samples examined had dried out considerably before they were received, as was evident from their mechanical condition, weight of package, etc.   In such cases the per cents given on the original sample are based on the goods as received and will not represent the correct composition of the material as placed on the market, on account of this decrease in the moisture content, making the per cent of the other constituents as given higher than they were originally

In making lead arsenate from lead acetate and disodium arsenate a certain amount of acetic acid is formed   This had not been completely washed out in all cases, as was shown by the fact that several of the samples had a strong odor of acetic acid   No quantitative determination was made of the amount, but as it would be driven off at the temperature of drying, the term "moisture" not only includes water, but any other material volatile at from 105° to 110° C

One of the samples examined was lead arsenite and another was a mixture of the arsenate and arsenite in about equal proportions Several others contained small amounts of arsenic as arsenite, but usually only traces were present   In such cases the water-soluble arsenic reported as arsenic oxid (As_2O_5) contained some arsenious oxid   As soluble arsenic is injurious in either form, the two have not been determined separately, except in the cases noted, where it was present entirely as arsenite

On inspecting the analyses given in Table I, the first striking fact that will be observed is the great variation in the composition of the different samples.   The content of arsenic oxid ranges from 6 03 to 43 81 per cent (the latter as As_2O_3); lead oxid varies from 23.06 to 72 57 per cent, moisture from 0 41 to 61 84 per cent, water-soluble arsenic from 0 02 to 5.45 per cent (As_2O_3), and water-soluble impurities from 0 08 to 7 54 per cent.

In order to secure a more uniform basis for comparison all of the determinations have been calculated to moisture-free material   A much greater uniformity is shown when this is done, but there is still a considerable variation.   Arsenic oxid ranges from 10 30 to 44 70 per cent (the latter As_2O_3), lead oxid from 49.58 to 77.93 per cent; water-soluble arsenic oxid from 0.03 to 5 56 per cent (As_2O_3); and water-soluble impurities from 0 14 to 13.86 per cent.

Evidently in some cases the salts formed as by-products in the manufacture have not been washed out, or at most the material has simply been run through the filter press to remove the superfluous liquid, as is shown by the high per cent of water-soluble material in a number of samples

Lead arsenate is recommended for spraying purposes mixed with water in various proportions   A standard formula and one frequently recommended is 2 pounds to 50 gallons   It is easy to see from the analyses of these samples that if they were made up according to this formula there would be in some cases eight times as much arsenic applied as in others   As a consequence the spraying might be condemned as inefficient in certain cases, owing to too weak an application, while in others, using the very same formula, severe injury to the tree might result from too strong an application.   Another and even more serious condition may result from a high per cent of soluble arsenic, due to the lead arsenate being carelessly or improperly made.   Where sufficient care is exercised in the making the soluble arsenic should certainly not exceed 0 75 of 1 per cent, calculated as arsenic oxid (As_2O_5) on a 50 per cent moisture basis, or 1 5 per cent on a moisture-free basis

Lead arsenate should be packed in air-tight packages, in order to keep it in a moist condition until ready for use   After it has once been dried it is much more difficult to keep it in suspension during spraying, which often results in an unequal application   This is the main reason for putting it up in a moist condition instead of in the dry state   Forty to fifty per cent of moisture is sufficient to preserve it in good condition, if it is kept in air-tight receptacles until used   In case a package is opened and only partly used, that remaining may be held over in good condition for the next spraying, by covering it with an inch or more of water   Lead arsenate should always be bought in original packages, which are plainly labeled; when purchased from a broken package, more or less risk is run of not getting true lead arsenate   Three instances have been found in which supposed "lead arsenate" was purchased from drug stores, which on analysis proved to be white arsenic (arsenious oxid)   The result of spraying this material on the peach or any other fruit tree would be disastrous.

While some of the firms are making a good product, this can not be said of all.   It was not to be expected, however, that a perfect product would be produced in all cases. especially as the material has not been manufactured until recently and evidently some have taken up · the business without proper knowledge of the subject   The product will no doubt be improved as its use and preparation become better understood

II. "HOME-MADE" LEAD ARSENATE AND THE CHEMICALS ENTERING INTO ITS MANUFACTURE.

INTRODUCTION

As has been previously noted, arsenate of lead was first proposed as an insecticide in 1892, but it was several years before it was used to any great extent.   This was not a product that could be obtained on the market at that time and it was therefore necessary for those using it to prepare their own supply   These conditions no longer exist, as there are at the present time twenty or more firms in different parts of the United States which manufacture it, and it is possible to procure it in almost any section of the country Only those brands should be accepted, however, which bear the guaranty of a reliable manufacturer on the package When such can not be obtained at a reasonable price, or if only a small amount is needed, it may be advantageously made at home by following the directions which are given herein Again, in some cases where a large quantity is to be used and the proper chemicals can be purchased at a reasonable price, a considerable saving might result by making it at home, but this would probably not be advisable as a general rule In the making of such a product there is always some risk due to poor chemicals, an incorrect formula, or carelessness in making The chemicals used in its preparation are sodium arsenate and either lead acetate or lead nitrate All of these can be easily obtained from druggists and are the cheapest compounds containing the necessary elements in a suitable form The wholesale prices of the technical grades of these chemicals at the present time are Lead acetate, $7\frac{1}{4}$ to 8 cents per pound, lead nitrate, $7\frac{3}{4}$ to $8\frac{1}{4}$ cents per pound, sodium arsenate, $5\frac{1}{2}$ to 6 cents per pound These salts all show some variation in their composition and at times this may be very great, particularly in the case of sodium arsenate, which is the salt used to supply the arsenic. Samples of these chemicals have been obtained in various parts of the country from druggists and other sources and subjected to analysis In the lead salts the total amount of lead oxid has been determined and in the sodium arsenate total arsenic oxid and chlorin These are the only substances which it is necessary to consider, as they are the ones that enter into the reaction

METHODS OF ANALYSIS

LEAD SALTS

Total lead oxid —This may be determined as sulphate by precipitating with sulphuric acid, or as oxid by precipitating with ammonia and ammonium carbonate and converting into the oxid by ignition. The details of these methods are given in works on quantitative analysis and both give satisfactory results

SODIUM ARSENATE.

Total arsenic oxid —Dissolve 2 grams of the sample in water and make volume up to 250 cc Heat 50 cc of this solution to about 80° C , add 3 grams of potassium iodid and 50 cc of concentrated hydrochloric acid Let stand fifteen minutes, cool, add approximately tenth-normal sodium thiosulphate solution just to disappearance of color caused by free iodin (The end point is easy to obtain without the use of starch.) Add immediately sodium carbonate until most of the acid is neutralized, then after all the sodium carbonate has been dissolved complete the neutralization with sodium bicarbonate, adding it in considerable excess. Add a few drops of starch indicator (made by boiling 1 gram of pure starch in 100 cc of water), and run in standard iodin solution till all arsenite has been oxidized to arsenate as will be shown by the appearance of the blue color. Calculate the amount of arsenic present in terms of arsenic oxid (As_2O_5) from the volume of the standard iodin solution required for the oxidation.

The strength of the standard iodin solution is determined by titrating against a solution containing a known amount of arsenious oxid, in the same manner.

Chlorin (Volhard's method).—Acidify with nitric acid 50 cc of the solution used for determining total arsenic, then add an excess of standard silver nitrate solution and make up to 200 cc. Filter through a dry filter and determine the excess of silver in 100 cc of the filtrate by titrating with standard ammonium sulphocyanate solution, using solution of ferric alum as indicator. Twice the amount of silver in this 100 cc portion, subtracted from the total amount added, will give the amount of silver equivalent to the chlorin in the 50 cc of the solution originally taken, from which the per cent of chlorin present may be calculated.

COMPOSITION OF LEAD ACETATE.

RESULTS OF ANALYSES.

In Table II are given the analyses of the samples of lead acetate examined. In column four is given the equivalent of the lead oxid found in crystallized lead acetate, $Pb(C_2H_3O_2)_2 3H_2O$, in order to show more clearly the relative value of the various samples for the purpose of making lead arsenate.

TABLE II.—*Composition of lead acetates.*

Serial number.	Grade.	Lead oxid (PbO).	Lead oxid calculated to crystallized lead acetate.a
		Per cent.	Per cent.
4546	White..........................	58.84	100.11
4650	White..........................	59.29	100.88
4626	Commercial....................	66.43	113.03
4719	White..........................	59.93	101.97
4718	Brown.........................	60.94	103.69
4538	Pure granulated...............	59.97	102.04
4544	Pure granulated...............	60.76	103.38
4545	Pure granulated...............	60.67	103.23
4627	Purified granulated..........	66.77	113.61
4655	Commercial....................	59.00	100.39
4539	Purified granulated..........	58.76	99.98
4540	Purified granulated..........	60.76	103.38
4645	Purified......................	60.34	102.67
4647	C. P. powdered................	65.24	111.00
4543	C. P. crystallized............	58.83	100.10
4537	Purified......................	59.37	101.02
4642	Commercial....................	63.59	108.20
4832	Commercial....................	61.43	104.52

a Formula, $Pb(C_2H_3O_2)_2 3H_2O$.

DISCUSSION.

Pure crystallized lead acetate contains theoretically 58 81 per cent of lead oxid and 14 25 per cent of water of crystallization   A number of these samples have lost much of their water of crystallization, as is shown by the high lead content   The commercial "brown" acetate of lead is cheaper than the pure crystallized salt and the samples examined contained more lead   For these reasons the technical grade is to be preferred rather than the pure salt for the preparation of lead arsenate   None of the samples examined contained impurities which would in any way decrease their value for this purpose   One hundred pounds of samples Nos 4626 and 4627 would be equivalent to over 113 pounds of the crystallized salt for this purpose, in addition to being cheaper per pound.

COMPOSITION OF LEAD NITRATE.

RESULTS OF ANALYSES.

The results for total lead oxid in the samples of lead nitrate analyzed are as follows

TABLE III -- *Composition of lead nitrates*

Serial number	Lead oxid (PbO)	Calculated to lead nitrate [Pb(NO_3)$_2$]
	Per cent	*Per cent*
a 4541	67 09	99 60
a 4550	67 03	99 51
b 4628	66 33	98 48
b 4654	66 19	98 27
a 4646	67 10	99 62

a "C P"
b "Commercial"

DISCUSSION

The theoretical per cent of lead oxid in pure lead nitrate is 67.35. It will be seen that all of these samples contain very close to this amount.   The composition of lead nitrate is more uniform than lead acetate, and it also contains more lead, though some of the partially dehydrated samples of the acetate contain nearly as much.

COMPOSITION OF SODIUM ARSENATE.

RESULTS OF ANALYSES

Pure crystallized sodium arsenate, or, chemically, disodium hydrogen arsenate, has the formula $Na_2HAsO_4 7H_2O$, and contains theoretically 36.84 per cent of arsenic oxid (As_2O_5).   One authority states that this salt has the composition $Na_2HAsO_4 12H_2O$, and gives directions for making lead arsenate based on this formula. This is misleading, as such a salt forms below 18° C.[a] (above this temperature it loses water rapidly) and it is not the ordinary sodium arsenate of commerce. The pure crystallized salt, however, is too expensive for the purpose in question and it is necessary to employ the technical grades. These are very cheap and if we can be assured of the absence of objectionable impurities they are just as good as the pure salt for making lead arsenate. In fact they usually contain more arsenic oxid than the crystallized salt, owing to the fact that they have been fused and do not contain water of crystallization, which theoretically amounts to 40.4 per cent in the pure salt. Frequently, however, they contain large amounts of impurities, usually sodium chlorid, which lowers the per cent of arsenic oxid. Sodium arsenate sold for technical purposes comes in varying degrees of purity, concerning which there has been much confusion. Two grades commonly on the market are the 50 per cent and the 65 per cent grades, which figures refer to the arsenic oxid (As_2O_5) content. In only one sample examined was the arsenic oxid over 45 per cent.

In Table IV is given the total arsenic oxid and chlorin in the samples of sodium arsenate examined.

TABLE IV.—*Composition of sodium arsenates.*

Serial number.	Arsenic oxid (As_2O_5).	Chlorin (Cl).
	Per cent.	*Per cent.*
4547	44.65	0.43
4649	68.07	.39
4625	44.59	12.58
4717	42.74	15.17
4548	37.39	.00
4623	37.23	.00
4831	37.08	.00
4549	37.29	.00
4653	39.33	17.72
4643	37.51	15.28
4542	37.11	.11

DISCUSSION.

All of the samples were tested for arsenic present as arsenite, but none was found except traces in two or three of the commercial samples. Nos. 4542, 4548, 4549, 4623, and 4831 are samples of the pure crystallized salt, and all of them have effloresced to a slight extent, which accounts for the arsenic content being a little above the theoretical amount. No. 4547 is comparatively pure and contains nearly 8 per cent more arsenic oxid than the crystallized salt, owing to partial dehydration. Nos. 4625, 4643, 4653, and 4717 are technical samples and are very impure, containing large amounts

---

[a] Fresenius, J. prakt. Chem., 1852, *56*:30.

of sodium chlorid, as shown by the high chlorin content On account of this, none of them is desirable for making lead arsenate. Sample No 4649 is a technical sample and is unusually high in arsenic oxid It is probably composed largely of sodium dihydrogen arsenate (NaH_2AsO_4)

The analyses here reported show that there is little or no risk in buying the technical grades of the lead salts, but sodium arsenate is much more variable, and when chlorin is present sufficient lead must be added to combine with this as well as with the arsenic This is a waste of the lead salt, as lead chlorid is not considered of value as an insecticide and therefore the presence of chlorids is objectionable, particularly in amounts greater than 3 or 4 per cent The presence of arsenious oxid (As_2O_3) or sodium arsenite is also objectionable, as by uniting with lead it forms lead arsenite, which is more soluble than the arsenate, does not remain in suspension as well, and, as shown by Kirkland and Burgess,[a] is less poisonous to insects

THEORETICAL COMPOSITION OF LEAD ARSENATE

As has been pointed out by others, arsenate of lead may mean any of the various lead arsenates, but the most common ones are the tri-plumbic arsenate and the plumbic hydrogen arsenate, represented by the formulas $Pb_3(AsO_4)_2$ and $PbHAsO_4$, respectively Most of the commercial samples consist of a mixture of these two, the one predominating depending upon the method used in its manufacture As has been shown by Smith[b] and Haywood,[c] when lead acetate and di-sodium arsenate are used for its preparation the following reaction takes place

$$3Pb(C_2H_3O_2)_23H_2O + 2Na_2HAsO_47H_2O = Pb_3(AsO_4)_2 + 4NaC_2H_3O_23H_2O + 2HC_2H_3O_2 + 11H_2O$$

Using nitrate of lead and di-sodium arsenate, Smith[d] gives the reaction thus:

$$5Pb(NO_3)_2 + 4Na_2HAsO_4(H_2O)^n = Pb_3(AsO_4)_2 + 2PbHAsO_4 + 8NaNO_3 + 2HNO_3 + n(H_2O).$$

Haywood[e] found the reaction to be mainly as follows.

$$Pb(NO_3)_2 + Na_2HAsO_47H_2O = PbHAsO_4 + 2NaNO_3 + 7H_2O$$

[a] Agriculture of Massachusetts, 1897, p 379
[b] Agriculture of Massachusetts, 1897, p 364
[c] U S Dept Agr , Bureau of Chemistry Bul 105, p 165
[d] Loc cit , p 365
[e] Loc cit , p 166

In numerous trials with pure salts it was found that the latter reaction occurs almost theoretically, though a small amount of the tri-plumbic arsenate is usually formed

With lead acetate, however, there are other conditions which affect the reaction, probably temperature, concentration, method of mixing, etc. In several cases when pure chemicals were used the resulting product was found to be principally the plumbic hydrogen arsenate. Most of the samples examined in which the acetate was used in the preparation consisted mainly of the tri-plumbic arsenate, $Pb_3(AsO_4)_2$. This contains theoretically 74 40 per cent of lead oxid (PbO), and 25 60 per cent of arsenic oxid (As_2O_5.)

As may be calculated from the reaction previously given, it will be found that by using pure crystallized lead acetate (58.81 per cent PbO) and crystallized sodium arsenate (36.84 per cent As_2O_5) there will be required to make 1 pound of tri-plumbic arsenate 1 296 pounds of lead acetate and 0 695 pound of sodium arsenate, or 64 55 per cent of lead acetate and 35 45 per cent of sodium arsenate

Plumbic hydrogen arsenate, $PbHAsO_4$, contains theoretically 64 26 per cent of lead oxid (PbO); 33 15 per cent of arsenic oxid (As_2O_5), and 2 59 per cent of water of constitution.

Calculating the amount of lead nitrate (67 35 per cent PbO), and sodium arsenate (36 84 per cent As_2O_5) required to make 1 pound of this compound from the second reaction given, the following result is obtained. 0 954 pound of lead nitrate, and 0 900 pound of sodium arsenate, or 51 43 per cent of lead nitrate, and, 48.57 per cent of sodium arsenate

However, formulas can not be given based on technical or even on pure salts, for a number of reasons

(1) Pure salts are too expensive to use
(2) The technical grades show considerable variation in composition, as has been shown
(3) Allowance must be made for other salt-forming compounds in the sodium arsenate notably chlorids which use up some of the lead salt
(4) The lead salt should be in slight excess to insure rendering all of the arsenic insoluble
(5) Under the varying conditions which exist at the time of making, the reactions do not proceed as indicated by theory

In regard to the last reason, it may be said that even if the exact chemical composition of the salts were known and the correct proportions calculated to satisfy the reaction were mixed together, it would seldom, if ever, result in a complete combination of the lead and arsenic radicals The only way to proceed, therefore, is either to add lead salt considerably in excess of the theoretical amount, or to add the lead salt gradually and test from time to time to see when it is in excess. The latter method is much the better one. In a few of the published formulas attention is called to the necessity of having the lead salt in excess, but in most of them no reference is made to this point. In the majority of the formulas, however, the amount called for is considerably in excess of the theoretical This, of course, results in a waste of the lead salt, except in rare instances, where sodium arsenate containing an unusually high per cent of arsenic is being used In such a case there might not be sufficient lead to combine with all of the arsenic, thus leaving the soluble arsenic salt in excess and yielding a product that would cause injury to most foliage to which it might be applied.

PUBLISHED FORMULAS.

A number of formulas for making lead arsenate have been published in the various experiment station bulletins, governmental reports, and works on economic entomology These, as a rule, call for lead acetate as the lead salt and show considerable variation in the relative proportion of the lead and arsenic salts. The various proportions which have been recommended are given below, with the number of publications in which they have appeared placed in parentheses The original proportion given by Moulton [a] and which was followed for the preparation of the arsenate of lead used by the Massachusetts gypsy moth commission, was sodium arsenate 29 93 per cent and lead acetate 70 07 per cent, or sodium arsenate 3 ounces and lead acetate 7 ounces This formula has been repeated in thirteen publications. Another proportion, recommended by Fernald [b] and found by the authors to have been more frequently recommended than any other (26 cases) is arsenate of soda 4 ounces and acetate of lead 11 ounces

The following formulas have also been found

Arsenate of soda Oz	Acetate of lead Oz
4	10 (1)
4	12 (1)
2⅜	7¼ (1)
6	18 (1)
8	24 (3)
10	25 (1)
10	24 (5)

Formulas using arsenate of soda and nitrate of lead have been given as follows.

Arsenate of soda Oz	Nitrate of lead Oz
5	10 (4)
12	18⅜ (1)
10	24 (3)

[a] Agriculture of Massachusetts, 1893, p 282
[b] Massachusetts Hatch Exper Sta , Bul 24.

The amount of water recommended to be added to these quantities varies from 16 to 200 gallons. In some cases one is directed to mix the chemicals, then add the water, in other cases to dissolve the chemicals in separate portions of water and then mix the solutions. But in only a few cases is attention called to the necessity of having the lead salt in excess or a method given for determining when it is in excess. The grade of arsenate of soda to be used is sometimes given, but usually no reference is made to it. The 4 to 11 formula is based on arsenate of soda of 50 per cent strength and the 3 to 7 formula on arsenate of soda of 65 per cent strength; that is, 50 per cent and 65 per cent of arsenic oxid (As_2O_3)

Some confusion seems to have arisen in regard to arsenate of soda and arsenite of soda, as some of the formulas call for the latter, though the other salt is no doubt intended. Arsenite of soda is not suitable for the purpose. In a few instances the objection to the presence of chlorids in the sodium arsenate is referred to, but usually this is not mentioned.

It was the practice originally to add glucose or thick molasses at the rate of 2 quarts to 100 gallons for the purpose of increasing the adhesive qualities of the mixture. This practice has since been discontinued, as it was found that these substances did not increase adhesion, nor was the material eaten any more readily when they were present.

According to some of the published formulas there would be present in the prepared mixture less than one-half pound of actual arsenate of lead to 150 gallons of water. It is very doubtful whether the application of such a small amount would be of sufficient benefit to pay for the trouble of applying it.

In all of the formulas the lead salt is present in large enough proportions, under ordinary conditions, to combine with all of the arsenic and still be in excess. In extreme cases, however, when sodium arsenate was used which contained an unusually large per cent of arsenic or of sodium chlorid this would not be true. It is necessary that a different formula should be used for different grades of chemicals, and unless the person making the lead arsenate knows the grade of material he is working with he will be in the dark as to which formula to employ. This shows how necessary it is to apply some test to determine when sufficient lead has been added, instead of using definite amounts of the two salts. The following tests for this purpose have been given.

After mixing the salts, filter a portion and to the clear filtrate add a few drops of dilute sulphuric acid, when, if lead is in excess, a white precipitate of lead sulphate will be formed. Instead of sulphuric acid, there may be added to the clear filtered liquid a few drops of chromate or dichromate of potash, when, if lead is in excess, a yellow precipitate of lead chromate will be formed If to a filtered portion of the solution a little of the lead acetate or lead nitrate solution is added and a white precipitate produced, it shows that the arsenic salt is still in excess and more lead should be added The objection to all of these tests is that the liquid must either be filtered or allowed to settle before the test can be applied, either of which takes considerable time and extra utensils for the purpose. The test described in the following directions for making lead arsenate has proven reliable and can be made instantaneously

DIRECTIONS FOR PREPARING LEAD ARSENATE

This method will give a good product, without any material waste of chemicals, and will require a minimum amount of time. For every pound of lead arsenate it is desired to make, use—

	Ounces
Formula A	
Sodium arsenate (65 per cent)..	8
Lead acetate (sugar of lead)...	22
Formula B	
Sodium arsenate (65 per cent)	8
Lead nitrate..	18

If the sodium arsenate employed is 50 per cent strength, use 10½ ounces instead of 8 Of the pure crystallized salt, 14 ounces would be required to furnish the same amount of arsenic oxid as would be furnished by the given amounts of the 50 and 65 per cent grades if they actually contained these per cents In only one technical sample examined, however, was the arsenic oxid content over 45 per cent The formulas are based on lead acetate containing 60 per cent of lead oxid and lead nitrate containing 66 per cent of lead oxid

Dissolve each salt separately in from 1 to 2 gallons of water [a] (they dissolve more readily in hot water), using wooden vessels After solution has taken place, pour slowly about three-fourths of the lead acetate or nitrate into the sodium arsenate Mix thoroughly and test the mixture by dipping into it a strip of potassium iodid test paper,[b] which will turn a bright yellow if lead is in excess If the paper does not turn yellow, add more of the lead salt slowly, stirring constantly, and test from time to time When the solution turns the paper yellow sufficient lead salt is present, but if it should occur that the paper does not turn yellow after all the lead salt has been added dissolve a little more and add until an excess is indicated The

---

[a] The solution of lead acetate may have a milky appearance This will be no objection, and it need not be filtered

[b] If potassium iodid test paper can not be obtained it may be prepared by dissolving a few crystals of potassium iodid in about a tablespoonful of water and saturating filter paper or blotting paper with this solution After the paper has dried, cut into strips and keep dry until needed

great advantage of this test is that it is not necessary to filter the solution or wait for it to settle.

If the paper is not at hand, the test may be made by adding a few drops of a solution of potassium iodid, when, if lead is in excess, the instant the drops touch the solution a bright yellow compound, lead iodid, will be formed.

It is very essential that the lead salt be added in *slight excess*, but a *large excess* should be avoided.

If the material has been carefully prepared with a good grade of chemicals it will not be necessary to filter and wash the lead arsenate formed, though it would be a safe precaution to allow the lead arsenate to settle, then decant the clear solution and discard it. Approximately 1 pound of actual lead arsenate will be obtained by using the amounts of chemicals specified, which is equivalent to practically 2 pounds of commercial lead arsenate in the paste form. It may be made up to 50 gallons with water if a formula is being used which calls for 2 pounds of commercial lead arsenate to 50 gallons, or if a stronger application is desired add less water.

As these chemicals are all extremely poisonous, vessels in which they have been dissolved or mixed should be plainly marked and not used for any other purpose.

COMPARATIVE MERITS OF LEAD ACETATE AND LEAD NITRATE.

As far as expense is concerned it makes little difference which of these lead salts is used, as their price per pound is practically the same. The nitrate may be slightly cheaper, as it contains a higher per cent of lead, though some of the commercial samples of lead acetate which are nearly free from moisture contain almost as much. A little less lead nitrate is required to make the same quantity of lead arsenate, since when made from this salt more of the lead hydrogen arsenate is formed, which contains a larger per cent of arsenic—on an average about 4 per cent more. This compound has also more desirable physical properties, as it remains in suspension better. Kirkland [a] has shown that the lead hydrogen arsenate is slightly more poisonous than the tri-plumbic arsenate. This may be due to the fact that the former has a larger per cent of arsenic and therefore a smaller quantity of it would give the same effect. It is probable, however, that the lead would possess some poisonous properties in this compound, and therefore the larger amount of lead in the one may somewhat offset the excess of arsenic in the other. Some have claimed that the lead hydrogen arsenate was more injurious to foliage than the tri-plumbic arsenate, but this was not found to be the case during the three years of the experiments here reported. Taking all of these

---

[a] Agriculture of Massachusetts, 1897, p. 386.

facts into consideration, it would appear from our knowledge at the present time that the product prepared from lead nitrate is slightly more desirable

PHYSICAL PROPERTIES OF LEAD ARSENATE

The physical properties or characteristics of all insecticides which are to be applied as a spray are very important   Freshly precipitated lead arsenate is a white, very light, flocculent compound, and it is hard to conceive of an insecticide possessing more desirable physical properties   When sprayed on foliage it forms a thin film over the leaf, and after once having been dried thereon it is with difficulty washed off by ordinary rains, and therefore need not be applied so frequently as some other insecticides   This is quite an important consideration, particularly as the greatest expense connected with spraying is the cost of applying the mixture

Another important point is the ease with which it may be kept in suspension in water. Such materials as Paris green, Scheele s green, and others which have a high specific gravity are with difficulty kept in suspension during spraying, and there is always great danger from the material becoming too concentrated in the bottom of the spray tank, thus causing too strong an application and resulting in the scorching of the foliage   Paris green is particularly objectionable in this regard, as it settles very rapidly unless thoroughly and constantly agitated   Lead arsenate shows considerable variation in the time of settling, depending upon the way in which it has been treated and also the chemicals from which it has been made   If it has once been dried, on mixing with water again it settles out much more readily than if it has never been dried   It is for this reason that is is generally put on the market in the form of a paste   There is also a difference between that prepared from lead nitrate and that prepared from lead acetate   The former is more bulky and remains in suspension much longer   After drying there is very little difference in rapidity of settling between the products made from the different lead salts   Plate I shows graphically the variation in settling observed among preparations of lead arsenate which have received different treatments   As stated in the legend, tube a is lead arsenate prepared from sodium arsenate and lead acetate, in tube b lead nitrate was used instead of the acetate, tubes c and d are the same as tubes a and b, respectively, except that they have been dried out and then mixed with water again   All of the samples represent the same amount of actual lead arsenate and the column of water in each case is 12 inches high   All were thoroughly shaken and then photographed, fig 1 after they had stood two minutes, and fig. 2 after they had stood fifty minutes   It will be noticed that after two minutes tube b had settled but very little, tube a about one-third of the way down, tube c nearly to the bottom, and tube d about halfway down   Some of the finer particles still remain in suspension in tubes c and d, and the distinguishing line between the water and the main body of the precipitate is indistinct.

After fifty minutes tube b is scarcely more than halfway down while the others have practically all settled to the bottom.

III. ACTION OF LEAD ARSENATE ON FOLIAGE.

GENERAL DISCUSSION

The fact is well known to entomologists, fruit growers, and others that the foliage of the stone fruits is very susceptible to injury by many substances used as insecticides and fungicides, notably arsenicals and Bordeaux mixture, when applied as a spray in sufficient strength to destroy insects and fungi. This is particularly true in regard to the peach, which seems to be the most delicate and easily injured of them all   For this reason entomologists have been endeavoring for many years to find an insecticide that would destroy leaf-eating insects and not injure the most delicate foliage.   The list of substances which may be used is somewhat limited, because of the fact that whatever the material may be it must be comparatively cheap and in such a physical condition as to be easily and thoroughly applied   There is no effective insecticide of this class known at the present time which can be used on the peach without more or less risk of injury   As a result of this condition, many peach growers have given up the use of arsenicals, and, in fact, in some sections many orchards have been abandoned entirely.   This is a serious problem, and if a successful method can be discovered of combating these destructive insects without injuring the tree or fruit it will mean millions of dollars to the peach industry   When lead arsenate was first used it was thought that it possessed all of the necessary qualifications and would prove to be the ideal insecticide   It is of inestimable value and is extensively used on apple and other more hardy foliage, and even on the peach it is often used without injury, as shown by many reports on the subject and as personally observed by the authors. Some of the statements in regard to this point which have appeared in several experiment station bulletins and other reports on the subject are quoted as follows. Fernald states that "it [arsenate of lead] can be used in large proportions, if necessary, even up to 25 pounds to 150 gallons of water, without injury to the foliage."[a]   "It does not injure the foliage of the most delicate plants, even when used in as large a proportion as 25 pounds, or even more, to 150 gallons of water."[b]   Marlatt "It may be used at any strength from 3 to 15

[a] Massachusetts Hatch Exper Sta , 1894, Bul 24, p 7

[b] Agriculture of Massachusetts, 1897, p 355

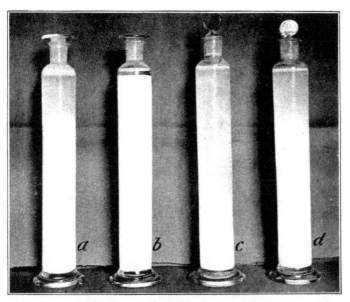

FIG. 1.—AFTER STANDING TWO MINUTES.

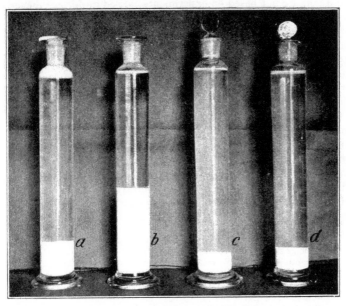

FIG. 2.—AFTER STANDING FIFTY MINUTES.

EFFECT OF DIFFERENT TREATMENTS ON THE SETTLING OF LEAD
ARSENATE.

a, Lead acetate used; *b*, lead nitrate used; *c* and *d*, same as *a* and *b*, but have been dried out

pounds to the 100 gallons of water without injury to foliage."[a] "It is totally without action on plants at any strength whatever, even when applied as a sirup."[b] Perkins [c] "It does no injury to the foliage" Smith. "This combination has the advantage of being harmless to foliage, whatever the strength in which it is applied * * * . Its great advantage is its harmlessness to plant life of all kinds"[d] "It is absolutely harmless to foliage at any strength * * * . It is the only effective poison of this character that can be safely applied to peach foliage and on conifers"[e] Stene [f] "It has the great advantage over most of our insecticides that it is entirely harmless to all plants in any strength" Bentley [g] "Arsenate of lead will not burn foliage" Taft and Shaw [h] "* * * it can be used upon the most tender foliage without injuring it, even though no lime is added" Green, Selby, and Gossard.[i] "* * * if properly made from good materials, will burn foliage but little, no matter what strength is used"

Others who have used and experimented with it have found that it frequently caused serious injury In some of the cases reported peach trees to which it was applied were practically entirely defoliated. There are a number of causes to which this variation in the observations of different investigators may be attributed. In the first place some of them are not based on experiments carried on for a sufficient length of time, or they have been conducted on apple or equally hardy foliage and the assumption made that the results would be the same on all foliage No doubt, also, arsenate of lead of poor quality and containing an unnecessarily large amount of arsenic in a water-soluble form has been used in some cases, which would result in burning. In view of the analyses reported in Table I, page 9, it would appear that this might easily occur. Making allowance for all of these conditions, however, it is still evident that injury results at times from the use of properly made lead arsenate, while the same experiments carried out in the same way at a different time or place may not result in any injury It is well known that the effect of insecticides and fungicides in general on plants shows great variation in different parts of the United States, and even in the same place in different years, depending upon the temperature, moisture, and undetermined influences Formulas that may be injurious to foli-

[a] U S Dept Agr , 1898, Farmers' Bul No 19, p 6
[b] Proc Seventh Ann Meeting, Assn Econ Ent , 1897, p 24
[c] Seventh Ann Rep , Vermont Agr Exper Sta , 1893, p 124
[d] Economic Entomology, 1896, p 437
[e] New Jersey Agr Exper Sta , 1903, Bul 169, p 8
[f] Rhode Island Agr Exper Sta , 1904, Bul 100, p 138
[g] Tennessee Agr Exper Sta Bul , 1905, vol 18 No 4, p 36
[h] Michigan Board of Agriculture, 1908, p 397
[i] Ohio Agr Exper Sta , 1908, Bul 199, p 94

age in some States may be used with safety in others. The injury
to foliage from arsenicals in arid regions is less than in non-arid
regions. Atmospheric conditions following spraying have a great
influence on the action of the spray mixture on the foliage. As to
why these conditions cause such variations in results no satisfactory
explanation has ever been given. It is well known to chemists that
pure arsenate of lead is practically insoluble in pure water, and it
seems impossible that it can cause injury as long as it remains so.
It has never been proven that leaves can absorb insoluble substances,
but investigators have shown conclusively that they do absorb salts
in solution. It would appear, therefore, that the lead arsenate must
be acted upon by some solvent, rendering more or less of the arsenic
soluble, before burning of the foliage will result. It was for the purpose of determining this important point, if possible, that this investigation was begun. In order that the experiments may be carried
out under the varying conditions presented by different seasons, it
is the intention to conduct them for a number of years in succession,
and while it is considered that the results obtained from the experiments conducted and reported herein are extremely suggestive they
are not given as conclusive, but on account of the importance of the
subject are presented as showing the progress that has been made.

PREPARATION OF THE LEAD ARSENATE USED.

That there might be no doubt of the purity of the lead arsenate
used, it was prepared in the laboratory from pure chemicals and
thoroughly washed. The product was then dried in order that it
might be more conveniently handled and accurately weighed.

No. 1 was made by adding a solution of crystallized lead acetate to
a solution of crystallized sodium arsenate until the lead salt was in
slight excess. The precipitated lead arsenate was allowed to settle,
the supernatant liquid decanted, then the material was washed by
decantation with pure water, and finally filtered and washed till the
greater portion of the soluble impurities were removed, after which
it was dried and powdered.

No. 2 was prepared in the same way, except that pure lead nitrate
was used instead of lead acetate. On analysis the samples showed
the following composition:

TABLE V.—*Analysis of lead arsenates prepared in the laboratory.*

Number of sample.	Moisture.	Total lead oxid (PbO).	Total arsenic oxid (As_2O_5).	Water-soluble impurities.	Water-soluble lead oxid (PbO).	Water-soluble arsenic oxid (As_2O_5).
	Per cent.	*Per cent.*	*Per cent.*	*Per cent.*	*Per cent.*	*Per cent.*
1	0.10	67.44	29.76	1.07	0.56	0.40
2	.09	64.02	32.64	1.57	.53	.49

Sample No 1 agrees closely in composition with a mixture, in about equal proportions, of tri-plumbic arsenate ($Pb_3(AsO_4)_2$) and plumbic hydrogen arsenate ($PbHAsO_4$), while No 2 corresponds very closely to the theoretical composition of plumbic hydrogen arsenate

EXPERIMENTAL WORK OF 1907

The experiments were carried out on trees in the Bureau of Entomology orchard on the Department farm at Arlington, Va. Two types of fruit trees were selected, namely, apple, which is one of the least susceptible to injury from arsenicals, and peach, which is the most tender and easily injured of all fruit foliage The only apple trees available for the experiments were young trees about 6 feet high, which had not reached the bearing age The peach trees were large and had borne several crops of fruit In applying the mixtures an ordinary barrel-sprayer outfit, fitted with a "Vermorel" double nozzle, was employed For each experiment there were used six apple and six peach trees These were divided into two sections A (three trees) received two applications and B (three trees) received three applications

DESCRIPTION OF EXPERIMENTS.

Experiment 1 —To test the effect of pure lead arsenate made from sodium arsenate and lead acetate Applied the material at the rate of 1½ pounds of dry lead arsenate to 50 gallons of water This is equivalent to about 2 pounds of a good grade of commercial lead arsenate to 50 gallons of water

Experiment 2 —Same as Experiment 1, except that freshly slaked quicklime was added at the rate of 4 pounds to 50 gallons of the spray mixture (To determine to what extent the presence of lime would lessen or prevent burning of the foliage)

Experiment 3 —Same as Experiment 1, except that lead nitrate instead of the acetate was used in the preparation of the lead arsenate (To show whether lead arsenate made from lead nitrate has a different action from lead arsenate made from lead acetate)

Experiment 4 —Same as Experiment 3, except that quicklime was added at the rate of 4 pounds to 50 gallons

Experiment 5 —To determine whether sodium acetate and acetic acid, which are formed as by-products when lead acetate acts on sodium arsenate, will scorch foliage Applied a mixture of sodium acetate and acetic acid in the proportion of 9 6 ounces of crystallized sodium acetate and 2 9 ounces of anhydrous acetic acid to 50 gallons of water (These are the respective amounts of sodium acetate and acetic acid obtained in the making of 1½ pounds of dry lead arsenate, assuming that tri-plumbic arsenate is formed)

Experiment 6 —To determine whether the amount of sodium acetate used in Experiment 5, when used alone, will injure foliage (Applied wash in the proportion of 9 6 ounces to 50 gallons)

Experiment 7 —To determine whether sodium nitrate, which is formed as a by-product when lead arsenate is made from sodium arsenate and lead nitrate, will injure foliage This was applied in the proportion of 10 4 ounces to 50 gallons of water, the theoretical amount of sodium nitrate formed in making 1½ pounds of dry lead arsenate, using lead nitrate and assuming that plumbic hydrogen arsenate is formed

Experiment 8.—To observe the effect of lead acetate on foliage to determine whether, if lead acetate were added in considerable excess, it would cause burning. Applied in the proportion of 2.7 ounces to 50 gallons of water. (This is 10 per cent of the theoretical amount of lead acetate required to make 1⅓ pounds of dry lead arsenate.)

Experiment 9.—To determine whether a still larger excess of lead acetate would burn when applied in the proportion of 5.4 ounces to 50 gallons of water. (This is 20 per cent of the amount required to make 1⅓ pounds of dry lead arsenate.)

Experiment 10.—To prove whether a small excess of lead nitrate would cause burning when applied in the proportion of 2.1 ounces to 50 gallons. (This is 10 per cent of the theoretical amount of lead nitrate required to make 1⅓ pounds of dry lead arsenate.)

Experiment 11.—Same as Experiment 10, except that the material was applied at the rate of 4.2 ounces to 50 gallons, which is 20 per cent of the theoretical amount of lead nitrate required to make 1⅓ pounds of dry lead arsenate.

A number of trees were left unsprayed in different portions of the orchard for comparison. The spraying was done on the following dates: April 18, first application on peach A and B, Experiments 1 to 7, inclusive. The following day it rained, and on April 20 the application was made according to Experiments 8 to 11, inclusive. The foliage on the apple trees had not developed sufficiently at this date to be sprayed. The second application was made on peach A and B and the first application on apple A and B on April 29 and 30. April 29 applied the spray in Experiments 1 to 9, inclusive, and on April 30 in Experiments 10 and 11. On May 13 and 14 the third application was made on peach B and the second application on apple A and B. On May 13 applied spray in Experiments 1 to 4, inclusive, and finished on the following day. The third application on apple B was made on June 4.

RECORD OF OBSERVATIONS.

Observations were made on the condition of the foliage at intervals of one to two weeks, and a detailed record kept which it is not necessary to record here in full. It may be stated in the first place in regard to the apple that no noticeable injury whatever was caused to the foliage from any of the various mixtures, either in the case of two or three applications. The following notes apply only to the peach:

June 4. On this date the last spraying was done and no evidence of any injury to the foliage was apparent which could be attributed to the materials previously applied. A number of leaves showed split and ragged edges, but this was no doubt caused by a severe hailstorm which occurred on May 19. No scorching or burning of the foliage was noticeable.

June 28. The foliage showed no injury except that on the trees in Experiment 11B, which had been sprayed three times with the stronger solution of lead nitrate. This showed some spotting and the "shot hole" effect, though the injury was not serious. The amount of fruit on these trees was small, many of them did not have any at all, and, owing to the unfavorable weather conditions which had prevailed during the growing season, the fruit was all of inferior quality; however, that on the unsprayed trees was in a worse condition than on those to which lead arsenate had been applied.

July 19. As far as the foliage was concerned, very little injury was apparent which could be attributed to the spraying mixtures. Experiment 3B showed slight leaf injury, some of the leaves showing the "shot hole" effect, but not more than 2 or 3 per cent were so injured. As before noted, the small amount of fruit present was, as a rule, inferior, but this condition appeared to be due mainly to fungus diseases. No fungicide had been applied, and the season was favorable to the growth of fungi.

August 7. No further injury was shown than that recorded in the preceding observations. A few peaches from trees sprayed with lead arsenate from either source had the appearance which arsenic injury frequently gives; that is, a dark, shriveled spot on the end, evidently where a drop of the spray had collected and concentrated. The greatest injury and in fact the only positive injury to foliage was shown in Experiments 11A and 11B, to which lead nitrate had been applied.

August 27. The fruit was just ripening at this date, but the crop was too small to draw any positive conclusions except in a general way. There was more fruit on the trees that had been sprayed with lead arsenate, and it was also in better condition. That on trees sprayed with lead acetate and lead nitrate was in very good condition, but the amount was small. The main difference in the appearance of the fruit that had received the applications of lead arsenate, aside from the few cases noted, was its deep red color, which gave it a better appearance and, in this instance, in no way injured the quality.

WEATHER CONDITIONS.

Table VI shows the meteorological conditions for the period from March 1 to September 1, 1907, and Table VII gives a comparison between the temperature and rainfall for this season and the average data for thirty-seven years.

TABLE VI.—*Monthly meteorological data, March to August, 1907, Washington, D. C.*

MARCH.

Date.	Temperature.			Precipitation.	Character of day.	Possible sunshine.
	Maximum.	Minimum.	Mean.			
	° F.	° F.	° F.	Inches.		Per cent.
1.....	40	31	36	0.26	Cloudy.....................	0
2.....	61	35	48	.19	Partly cloudy...............	65
3.....	50	28	39	Trace.	....do......................	38
4.....	44	26	35	Trace.	Clear......................	90
5.....	45	30	38	.02	Partly cloudy..............	36
6.....	40	28	34	.00	Clear......................	91
7.....	28	22	25	.02	Cloudy....................	3
8.....	48	28	38	.08	Partly cloudy..............	40
9.....	51	33	42	Trace.	....do......................	74
10....	35	29	32	.00	Cloudy....................	0
11....	44	27	36	Trace.	Clear.....................	83
12....	44	26	35	.17	Cloudy....................	0
13....	71	43	57	.03	......do....................	8
14....	73	40	56	.08	......do....................	6
15....	55	36	46	.01	Clear.....................	89
16....	62	31	46	.00	......do....................	96
17....	70	38	54	.00	......do....................	77
18....	61	44	52	Trace.	Partly cloudy..............	75
19....	54	40	47	.81	Cloudy....................	0
20....	58	42	50	.01	Clear......................	100
21....	55	32	44	.00	Partly cloudy..............	45
22....	90	40	65	.00	......do....................	75
23....	93	56	74	.00	......do....................	84
24....	85	48	66	.00	Clear......................	80
25....	56	39	48	.00	......do....................	75
26....	66	37	52	.00	Cloudy....................	41
27....	80	46	63	.00	......do....................	70
28....	83	54	68	.00	Partly cloudy..............	60
29....	92	55	74	.00	Clear......................	98
30....	74	56	65	.00	......do....................	81
31....	56	41	48	.21	Cloudy....................	0
Mean or total.	60.1	37.5	48.8	2.79		

TABLE VI.—*Monthly meteorological data, March to August, 1907, Washington, D. C.*—
Continued.

APRIL.

Date.	Temperature.			Precipi-tation.	Character of day.	Possible sunshine.
	Maxi-mum.	Mini-mum.	Mean.			
	°F.	°F.	°F.	Inches.		Per cent.
1....	45	29	37	Trace.	Partly cloudy............	69
2....	48	23	36	0.00	Clear................	100
3....	65	29	47	.00	....do...........	100
4....	72	36	54	Trace.	Partly cloudy............	88
5....	74	46	60	Trace.	....do...........	57
6....	45	32	38	.12	Cloudy.............	3
7....	40	32	36	.34	....do...........	0
8....	59	39	49	.07	Partly cloudy......	41
9....	49	34	42	1.06	....do...........	34
10....	47	38	42	Trace.	....do...........	62
11....	53	36	44	.00	....do...........	79
12....	46	37	42	.01	Cloudy.............	33
13....	49	39	44	.00	....do...........	33
14....	44	35	40	.00	Partly cloudy......	47
15....	51	33	42	.00	Clear................	100
16....	65	37	51	.00	Partly cloudy......	54
17....	48	38	43	.00	....do...........	83
18....	57	34	46	.00	....do...........	80
19....	48	38	43	.21	Cloudy.............	8
20....	54	35	44	.00	Partly cloudy......	66
21....	58	33	46	.00	Clear................	100
22....	65	35	50	.00	Partly cloudy......	71
23....	61	51	56	1.23	Cloudy.............	4
24....	65	47	56	Trace.	Clear................	100
25....	79	40	60	.00	....do...........	92
26....	83	57	70	.49	....do...........	75
27....	61	46	54	.08	Partly cloudy......	69
28....	59	48	54	.00	Cloudy.............	22
29....	71	52	62	Trace.	Partly cloudy......	55
30....	78	55	66	.00	Cloudy.............	53
Mean or total.	58.0	38.8	48.4	3.61		

MAY.

Date.	Maxi-mum.	Mini-mum.	Mean.	Precipi-tation.	Character of day.	Possible sunshine.
1....	68	51	60	0.61	Cloudy.............	0
2....	60	48	54	.00	....do...........	9
3....	65	49	57	Trace.	Partly cloudy......	49
4....	70	46	58	.13	Clear................	69
5....	62	39	50	.00	....do...........	100
6....	71	51	61	.52	Cloudy.............	10
7....	62	57	60	Trace.	....do...........	0
8....	71	52	62	.48	Clear................	70
9....	67	54	60	.24	Cloudy.............	18
10....	78	52	65	Trace.	Clear................	85
11....	62	42	52	.05	....do...........	75
12....	59	39	49	.00	....do...........	100
13....	73	44	58	.00	....do...........	100
14....	85	51	68	.00	....do...........	100
15....	83	59	71	.01	Partly cloudy......	73
16....	70	57	64	.39	Cloudy.............	0
17....	70	54	62	.00	Partly cloudy......	51
18....	83	53	68	Trace.	Clear................	76
19....	84	62	73	1.10	Partly cloudy......	51
20....	67	50	58	.10	....do...........	34
21....	60	41	50	.00	Clear................	100
22....	70	39	54	.00	....do...........	86
23....	74	56	65	.01	Cloudy.............	20
24....	66	56	61	.23	....do...........	12
25....	58	46	52	.14	....do...........	4
26....	61	46	54	.20	....do...........	0
27....	72	51	62	.58	Partly cloudy......	35
28....	64	44	54	.00	Clear................	87
29....	72	42	57	.00	....do...........	79
30....	74	49	62	.00	....do...........	100
31....	61	52	56	.24	Cloudy.............	0
Mean or total.	69.1	49.4	59.2	5.03		

TABLE VI.—*Monthly meteorological data, March to August, 1907, Washington, D. C.*—Continued.

JUNE.

Date.	Temperature.			Precipitation.	Character of day.	Possible sunshine.
	Maximum.	Minimum.	Mean.			
	°F.	°F.	°F.	Inches.		Per cent.
1.....	54	49	52	2.20	Cloudy	0
2.....	53	48	50	.14	.....do	0
3.....	69	49	59	.00	Partly cloudy	53
4.....	70	46	58	Trace.	Clear	65
5.....	77	56	66	.16	Partly cloudy	62
6.....	74	53	64	.00	Clear	80
7.....	73	50	62	.11	.....do	69
8.....	65	54	60	.21	Cloudy	20
9.....	76	50	63	.00	Clear	100
10....	71	52	62	Trace.	.....do	69
11....	57	50	54	.81	Cloudy	0
12....	62	50	56	.05	.....do	1
13....	59	52	56	.09	.....do	3
14....	62	55	58	.07	.....do	0
15....	82	51	66	.00	Clear	64
16....	81	55	68	.00	.....do	100
17....	86	55	70	.00	.....do	100
18....	82	57	70	.00	.....do	66
19....	81	61	71	Trace.	Partly cloudy	48
20....	83	61	72	.00	.....do	40
21....	88	66	77	.00	Clear	100
22....	89	64	76	.00	.....do	78
23....	85	66	76	.00	Partly cloudy	52
24....	88	70	79	Trace.	Clear	65
25....	89	72	80	.01	.....do	79
26....	87	71	79	.06	.....do	69
27....	82	61	72	.00	.....do	87
28....	83	56	70	.01	Partly cloudy	64
29....	68	61	64	.94	Cloudy	70
30....	77	59	68	.00	Partly cloudy	32
Mean or total.	75.1	56.7	65.9	4.86		

JULY.

Date.	Maximum.	Minimum.	Mean.	Precipitation.	Character of day.	Possible sunshine.
1.....	86	59	72	0.27	Clear	85
2.....	85	65	75	.00	Partly cloudy	74
3.....	77	58	68	.00	Clear	97
4.....	81	52	66	.00	.....do	84
5.....	81	57	69	Trace.	Partly cloudy	68
6.....	86	63	74	.00	Clear	84
7.....	90	66	78	Trace.	.....do	88
8.....	93	73	83	.00	.....do	67
9.....	85	72	78	Trace.	Partly cloudy	54
10....	91	68	80	.02	.....do	57
11....	93	70	82	Trace.	.....do	68
12....	82	68	75	.04	Cloudy	18
13....	80	63	72	.00	Partly cloudy	65
14....	84	61	72	.00	.....do	83
15....	82	64	73	.00	.....do	35
16....	88	72	80	Trace.	Cloudy	61
17....	85	73	79	.31	.....do	36
18....	91	74	82	Trace.	.....do	36
19....	87	72	80	Trace.	Partly cloudy	56
20....	90	74	82	Trace.	.....do	57
21....	83	66	74	.00	Clear	100
22....	87	62	74	Trace.	Partly cloudy	80
23....	88	71	80	.00	Clear	82
24....	91	69	80	.00	.....do	83
25....	92	71	82	.02	Partly cloudy	76
26....	86	69	78	Trace.	Cloudy	43
27....	80	61	70	.00	Clear	97
28....	83	62	72	.00	Partly cloudy	55
29....	72	65	68	.89	Cloudy	0
30....	86	65	76	.00	Clear	99
31....	85	63	74	.00	.....do	100
Mean or total.	85.5	66.1	75.8	1.55		

TABLE VI.—*Monthly meteorological data, March to August, 1907, Washington, D.C.*—
Continued.

AUGUST.

Date.	Temperature.			Precipi-tation.	Character of day.	Possible sunshine.
	Maxi-mum.	Mini-mum.	Mean.			
	° F.	° F.	° F.	Inches.		Per cent.
1.....	87	66	76	0.00	Partly cloudy...............	42
2.....	89	67	78	.00	Clear.....................	84
3.....	78	62	70	.79	Cloudy...................	24
4.....	78	58	68	.01	Clear.....................	100
5.....	79	59	69	.12	Cloudy...................	20
6.....	88	67	78	.43	Partly cloudy.............	59
7.....	89	67	78	.00	Clear.....................	75
8.....	91	67	79	.00	.....do..................	81
9.....	76	66	71	.67	Cloudy...................	0
10....	76	66	71	.40	.....do..................	9
11....	80	70	75	.00	.....do..................	36
12....	88	67	78	.00	Clear.....................	72
13....	85	71	78	.09	Partly cloudy.............	61
14....	77	62	70	.00	Clear.....................	74
15....	79	56	68	.00	.....do..................	100
16....	76	66	71	Trace.	Cloudy...................	7
17....	88	68	78	Trace.	Partly cloudy.............	57
18....	80	65	72	.04	Cloudy...................	6
19....	81	60	70	.00	Clear.....................	99
20....	82	70	76	.70	Partly cloudy.............	84
21....	88	67	78	.20	.....do..................	55
22....	73	58	66	Trace.	.....do..................	39
23....	72	56	64	.64	Cloudy...................	0
24....	86	67	76	.25	Partly cloudy.............	79
25....	78	66	72	.00	Clear.....................	99
26....	81	55	68	.00	.....do..................	98
27....	77	58	68	Trace.	Cloudy...................	10
28....	80	63	72	.00	Partly cloudy.............	34
29....	78	60	69	.00	Clear.....................	100
30....	80	57	68	Trace.	Partly cloudy.............	21
31....	80	59	70	.00	.....do..................	66
Mean or to-tal.	81.3	63.4	72.4	4.34		

TABLE VII.—*Comparison of monthly meteorological data for 1907 with the average for thirty-seven years.*

Month.	Temperature.			Rainfall.		
	Mean for 1907.	Mean for thirty-seven years.	Average daily excess or defi-ciency as compared with mean for thirty-seven years.	Total for 1907.	Mean for thirty-seven years.	Monthly excess or deficiency as com-pared with mean for thirty-seven years.
	° F.	° F.	° F.	Inches.	Inches.	Inches.
March......	48.8	42.2	+6.6	2.79	3.97	−1.18
April......	48.4	52.9	−4.5	3.61	3.19	+0.42
May........	59.2	64.0	−4.8	5.03	3.75	+1.28
June.......	65.9	73.0	−7.1	4.86	4.14	+0.72
July.......	75.8	76.9	−1.1	1.55	4.64	−3.09
August.....	72.4	75.0	−2.6	4.34	4.41	−0.07

SUMMARY FOR 1907.

Summing up the results for the season it can be stated that no injury resulted to the foliage of the apple from any of the mixtures applied, and only very slight injury to that of the peach, none of which was of a decided enough character to attribute it with certainty to the spraying Some of the trees which had not been sprayed at all showed a condition which would have been attributed to spraying injury if it had not been known that no insecticide had been applied to them The most positive results were shown on trees which had received the applications of lead nitrate, but the fruit on these trees did not appear to have been injured in the least By referring to the meteorological report for the period several striking facts will be noticed March, the month preceding spraying, was unusually warm, the mean being 6 6° higher than the average of the month for the preceding thirty-seven years, and also higher than for the month following This caused the trees to put out their foliage very early Following this the temperature was below normal for the entire growing season to the following extent April 4 5°, May 4 8°, June 7 1°, July 1 1°, and August 2 6° below the daily average for these months for the preceding thirty-seven years The rainfall for April, May, and June—the months when spraying was actually done—was considerably above the average, and the number of clear days for this period was only about one in three In every case rain fell on the same day or within two days after spraying These abnormal conditions render the drawing of any satisfactory conclusions from this year's work impossible The recorded experience of users of Paris green, other arsenicals, and Bordeaux mixture shows that greater injury has occurred following wet weather This may be true in general, but when spraying is followed soon thereafter by heavy rain the material may be washed off to such an extent that injury would not result from the small amount remaining Frequent rains which are just sufficient to thoroughly wet the foliage would naturally produce conditions favorable to the maximum injury

EXPERIMENTAL WORK OF 1908.

DESCRIPTION OF EXPERIMENTS

The results obtained in 1907 indicated that it was not necessary to continue experiments with two applications; therefore in 1908 three applications were made in all except one instance, to which attention is called later The experiments were conducted on the same apple trees as in the preceding year, but conditions made it necessary to select peach trees in another orchard These were young vigorous trees and were in their second bearing year As they were not large, a five-gallon knapsack sprayer outfit was selected for the work as being more convenient.

All of the experiments made in 1907 were repeated this year with the following in addition:

Experiment 12.—To test the effect of applying lead arsenate made from lead acetate and sodium arsenate without removing any of the by-products formed; i. e., sodium acetate, acetic acid, and a slight excess of lead acetate.

Experiment 13.—Same as Experiment 12, except that lime was added in the proportion of 4 pounds to 50 gallons.

Experiment 14.—To test the effect of lead arsenate made from lead nitrate and sodium arsenate without removing the by-products formed; i. e., sodium nitrate and a slight excess of lead nitrate.

Experiment 15.—Same as Experiment 14, except that lime was added at the rate of 4 pounds to 50 gallons.

In these four experiments the lead arsenate was applied in the same proportion as in other experiments in which it was used; that is, on the basis of $1\frac{1}{3}$ pounds of dry material to 50 gallons of water.

Four apple and four peach trees were used for each experiment. The first application was made on April 27 and the second on May 8. On May 20 the third application was made on the apple trees and Experiments 1 to 4 on the peach, when work was interrupted by a very heavy rain (1.86 inches), followed by several days of unsettled weather. On the 25th the remaining mixtures were applied, and Experiments 1 to 4 were resprayed. The latter, therefore, had received four applications of lead arsenate, but as the third had not had sufficient time to dry completely on the leaves before rain fell it was undoubtedly largely washed off. The last application was followed by five days of very hot, clear weather without rain.

RECORD OF OBSERVATIONS.

When the last spraying was done, on May 25, there was no injury apparent from any of the applications previously made. June 4 no injury could be observed to any of the apple trees. The foliage of the peach, however, showed very decided injury in some cases, as noted below.

NOTES MADE ON JUNE 4.

Experiment 1.—Quite a number of leaves had brown, shriveled edges and showed the "shot hole" effect, the injury, however, not being severe. Experiments 2, 3, and 4 the same, accompanied in the latter case by slight dropping and yellowing of the leaves.

Experiment 5.—Evidence of very slight injury; Nos. 6, 7, and 8, no injury.

Experiment 9.—Slight injury, some "shot-hole" effect; no dropping of leaves.

Experiment 10.—Same as No. 9.

Experiment 11.—Same as Experiment 9, but more severe; some dropping of leaves.

Experiment 12.—Showed some injury; leaves pretty badly spotted, and some had dropped.

Experiment 13.—Same as Experiment 12, but not so severe.

FIG. 1.—LEAVES FROM TREES IN EXPERIMENT 3. (NATURAL SIZE.)

FIG. 2.—LEAVES FROM TREES IN EXPERIMENT 12. (REDUCED.)

PEACH LEAVES SHOWING INJURY FROM LEAD ARSENATE.

Experiment 14 —A few leaves had fallen, but the injury was less marked than in Experiment 12

Experiment 15 —Practically the same as Experiment 14

Plate II, fig 1, shows the appearance of leaves on June 4, injured by lead arsenate These were selected from trees in Experiment 3 as representative Figure 2 shows some of the most severely injured leaves taken from Experiment 12.

NOTES MADE ON JUNE 9

Apple trees showed no injury • The notes on the peach trees were as follows

Experiment 1 —Considerable injury to foliage, a great many leaves had fallen, as evidenced by the thin appearance of the foliage and the number of leaves on the ground

Experiment 2 —Injury very evident, but not so severe as in Experiment 1 A few leaves had fallen

Experiment 3 —Many leaves with "shot holes," but as a whole the injury appeared to be slightly less than in Experiment 1

Experiment 4 —Practically the same as Experiment 2, except that a few more leaves had fallen

Experiment 5 —A little "shot holing" of leaves, but none had fallen As a whole the trees looked healthy and in good condition

Experiment 6 —No injury noticeable

Experiment 7 —Foliage in good condition, fine green color, no injury

Experiment 8 —No injury

Experiment 9 —Injury slight, a few "shot holes," no fallen leaves

Experiment 10 —Same as Experiment 9

Experiment 11 —Some injury, many leaves with numerous "shot holes," but few had fallen

Experiment 12 —Quite severely injured Many fallen leaves and foliage noticeably thin on tree Many leaves were yellow and had numerous "shot holes "

Experiment 13 —Considerable injury, but not so severe as in Experiment 12 Not many yellow leaves

Experiment 14 —Practically the same as Experiment 12

, *Experiment 15* —Same as Experiment 13

NOTES MADE ON JULY 29 ON CONDITION OF FRUIT

Apple foliage uninjured, no fruit Notes on the peach trees were as follows.

Experiment 1 —Fruit nearing maturity, very much redder in color than that on trees not sprayed with arsenicals Many peaches, approximately 40 per cent, showed the injurious effect of spraying by having a brown or black shriveled spot usually around or near the stem end or on the upper side In some cases the injury showed on the small end, when the fruit was hanging down, presumably a drop of the liquid having collected there and concentrated

Experiment 2 —Same as Experiment 1, injury not so severe

Experiment 3 —Same as Experiment 1, no more severe

Experiment 4 —Same as Experiment 2

Experiment 5 —Fruit normal color (green), not injured from spraying

Experiments 6, 7, and 8 --Same as No 5

Experiments 9, 10, and 11 —Fruit in good condition, normal color

Experiment 12 —Injury about the same as in Experiment 1 but not so severe, a smaller per cent of injured fruit, probably not over 30

Experiment 13 — Fruit deep red in color, as was all that sprayed with lead arsenate, not over 10 per cent showed injured spots and these were not so large nor deep as in Experiment 12

Experiment 14 — Injury practically the same as in Experiment 12

Experiment 15 — Fruit not so red, injury about the same as Experiment 13

The presence of lime showed some beneficial effect by lessening the injury to the fruit as well as to the foliage The fruit on unsprayed trees was still deep green in color and about one week behind that sprayed with lead arsenate as to maturity All trees were in a healthy looking condition aside from the fact that Experiments 1 to 4 and 12 to 15, inclusive, were not so thickly foliated, owing to previous dropping of the leaves The fruit on these trees, in addition to being a deep red, was more fully matured, and ripened about a week earlier than that unsprayed

Plate III shows the trees on the unsprayed plot with normal healthy foliage Plate IV represents a tree in Experiment 12 sprayed with lead arsenate and showing partial defoliation, leaving the fruit largely exposed Most of the leaves on the ends of the branches came out after the spraying was done, thus masking to a large extent the injury produced

NOTES MADE ON AUGUST 13 ON CONDITION OF FRUIT

These observations on the peach crop may be generalized Experiments 1 to 4, inclusive, and 12 to 15, inclusive, in which lead arsenate had been applied, showed about 50 per cent of injured fruit when no lime was used and about 25 per cent injured when lime was applied That showing the worst injury was somewhat shriveled and usually dropped before having fully matured In other cases it showed a dark shriveled spot, usually around the stem end, but frequently on the upper side or on the small end This condition is brought out in fig 1, which shows some of the most seriously injured fruit that remained on the trees The per cent of insect injury, as shown by wormy fruit, was very small, in no case over 5 per cent of the total

Experiment 9, in which lead acetate was used, yielded more perfect fruit than any of the other trees sprayed, 90 per cent of it was sound, 80 per cent of which was of good size and practically perfect, while 10 per cent showed insect injury.

CHECK PLOT, NOT SPRAYED, SHOWING NORMAL, HEALTHY FOLIAGE OF PEACH TREES.

PLATE IV.

PEACH TREE IN EXPERIMENT 12 SPRAYED WITH LEAD ARSENATE AND SHOWING PARTIAL

The fruit from all of the other sprayed trees was in practically the same condition as that from the unsprayed trees, none of the mixtures having lessened insect injury except lead nitrate, which was effective to a slight extent. Fruit from the unsprayed trees was very much gummed; from 50 to 60 per cent was wormy, and not over 30 per cent was sound and marketable.

FIG. 1.—Injured peaches from trees sprayed with lead arsenate. (Reduced.)

WEATHER CONDITIONS.

The tables following give the meteorological conditions for the period from March 1 to September 1, 1908, and a comparison of the average data for thirty-eight years with those for the season of 1908.

LEAD ARSENATE.

TABLE VIII.—*Monthly meteorological data, March to August, 1908, Washington, D. C.*

MARCH.

Date.	Temperature.			Precipi-tation.	Character of day.	Possible sunshine.
	Maxi-mum.	Mini-mum.	Mean.			
	°F.	°F.	°F.	Inches.		Per cent.
1....	35	30	32	0.20	Cloudy......................	0
2....	55	32	44	.02	.....do......................	4
3....	48	32	40	.00	Partly cloudy...............	81
4....	46	26	36	.00	Clear.......................	85
5....	41	26	34	.10	Cloudy.....................	4
6....	38	34	36	.59	.....do......................	0
7....	64	37	50	.00	Clear.......................	100
8....	56	31	44	.00	Partly cloudy...............	66
9....	45	33	39	.27	Cloudy.....................	0
10..	52	27	40	.00	Clear.......................	100
11..	61	33	47	.00	Partly cloudy...............	86
12....	66	44	55	Trace.	Clear.......................	100
13..	66	36	51	.00	Partly cloudy...............	86
14..	66	47	56	Trace.	Clear.......................	100
15....	74	45	60	.04	Cloudy.....................	34
16...	62	41	52	Trace.	Partly cloudy...............	72
17....	49	39	44	Trace.	.....do......................	4
18....	51	42	46	Trace.	Cloudy.....................	10
19...	66	38	52	.21	Partly cloudy...............	45
20....	38	30	34	.00	Cloudy.....................	11
21....	46	25	36	.00	Clear.......................	100
22....	56	32	44	Trace.	Partly cloudy...............	75
23...	56	47	52	.32	Cloudy.....................	0
24....	65	46	56	.00	Partly cloudy...............	65
25....	57	41	49	.00	.....do......................	68
26....	75	40	58	.00	Clear.......................	88
27....	80	58	69	.00	.....do......................	90
28....	73	62	68	.05	Cloudy.....................	6
29....	73	43	58	.35	.....do......................	18
30....	52	40	46	.00	.....do......................	41
31....	50	42	46	.30	.....do......................	0
Mean or to-tal ..	56.8	38.0	47.4	2.45		

APRIL.

1.....	51	44	48	0.08	Cloudy......................	0
2.....	63	38	50	.21	Partly cloudy...............	45
3.....	41	32	36	Trace.	.....do......................	59
4.....	51	33	42	.00	.....do......................	95
5.....	53	29	41	.03	.....do......................	7
6.....	69	48	58	.00	Clear.......................	91
7.....	77	44	60	.00	.....do......................	88
8.....	75	58	66	.43	Cloudy.....................	12
9.....	70	43	56	.07	Partly cloudy...............	86
10....	53	40	46	.15	Cloudy.....................	0
11....	69	46	58	.01	Partly cloudy...............	74
12....	62	41	52	.00	Clear.......................	100
13....	78	40	59	.00	.....do......................	91
14....	60	40	50	.00	.....do......................	91
15....	64	47	56	.28	Cloudy.....................	0
16....	63	38	50	.01	Clear.......................	82
17....	57	35	46	.00	.....do......................	100
18....	60	44	52	.10	Cloudy.....................	4
19....	72	51	62	Trace.	Partly cloudy...............	57
20....	80	44	62	.00	Clear.......................	100
21....	60	43	52	.00	.....do......................	100
22....	76	39	58	.00	.....do......................	100
23....	83	55	69	.00	.....do......................	94
24....	87	54	70	.00	.....do......................	92
25....	76	57	66	.02	Partly cloudy...............	47
26....	85	58	72	.00	Clear.......................	100
27....	85	65	75	.03	Partly cloudy...............	64
28....	71	56	64	.00	.....do......................	65
29....	76	46	61	.00	Clear.......................	93
30....	68	42	55	.17	Partly cloudy...............	44
Mean or to-tal ..	67.8	45.0	56.5	1.59		

TABLE VIII.—*Monthly meteorological data, March to August, 1908, Washington, D. C.*—Continued.

MAY.

Date.	Temperature.			Precipi-tation.	Character of day.	Possible sunshine.
	Maxi-mum.	Mini-mum.	Mean.			
	° F.	° F.	° F.	Inches.		Per cent.
1.....	56	39	48	0.00	Clear......................	92
2.....	66	44	55	.04	Partly cloudy.............	82
3.....	62	44	53	.00	....do....................	84
4.....	52	42	47	.29	Cloudy....................	3
5.....	55	45	50	.32	....do....................	9
6.....	50	46	48	.35	....do....................	0
7.....	64	47	56	1.01	....do....................	2
8.....	64	51	58	Trace.	Partly cloudy.............	42
9.....	60	49	54	.04	....do....................	55
10....	64	44	54	.00	Clear.....................	100
11....	82	42	62	.00	....do....................	100
12....	88	63	76	Trace.	Partly cloudy.............	52
13....	87	61	74	Trace.	....do....................	83
14....	88	58	73	.06	....do....................	55
15...	58	52	55	.13	Cloudy....................	0
16....	63	51	57	.01	Partly cloudy.............	7
17....	80	58	69	.00	....do....................	56
18....	78	60	69	Trace.	....do....................	69
19....	74	61	68	1.20	Cloudy....................	12
20....	81	61	71	1.86	....do....................	40
21....	75	64	70	Trace.	Partly cloudy.............	24
22....	84	64	74	Trace.	....do....................	69
23....	81	66	74	.05	....do....................	54
24....	85	63	74	.00	....do....................	81
25....	87	64	76	.00	Clear.....................	82
26....	88	68	78	.00	....do....................	79
27....	89	69	79	.00	....do....................	87
28....	92	67	80	.00	....do....................	99
29....	82	70	76	.00	Partly cloudy.............	60
30....	83	66	74	.74	....do....................	59
31....	85	64	74	.00	....do....................	86
Mean or to-tal ..	74.3	56.2	65.2	6.10		

JUNE.

1.....	72	59	66	0.00	Clear.....................	97
2.....	80	56	68	.00	....do....................	99
3.....	74	58	66	.09	Partly cloudy.............	66
4.....	67	58	62	.46	Cloudy....................	9
5.....	78	57	68	.00	Clear.....................	72
6.....	68	59	64	.00	Cloudy....................	7
7.....	81	52	66	.00	Partly cloudy.............	82
8.....	85	59	72	.00	Clear.....................	99
9.....	87	64	76	.02	....do....................	82
10....	82	65	74	Trace.	Partly cloudy.............	74
11...	73	61	67	.02	....do....................	30
12....	82	56	69	.00	Clear.....................	99
13....	84	58	71	.00	....do....................	100
14....	84	66	75	.00	....do....................	99
15....	78	58	68	1.00	Cloudy....................	29
16....	74	54	64	.00	Clear.....................	99
17....	75	52	64	.00	Partly cloudy.............	100
18....	78	58	68	.00	....do....................	70
19....	88	60	74	.00	Clear.....................	99
20....	89	70	80	.00	Partly cloudy.............	60
21....	89	70	80	Trace.	....do....................	83
22....	89	68	78	.00	....do....................	91
23....	94	68	81	.00	Clear.....................	88
24....	97	76	86	.00	....do....................	88
25....	85	71	78	.01	Partly cloudy.............	64
26....	80	64	72	.00	....do....................	85
27....	83	57	70	.08	Clear.....................	76
28....	85	57	71	.00	....do....................	93
29....	92	67	80	.00	Partly cloudy.............	99
30....	87	71	79	.05	Clear.....................	72
Mean or to-tal ..	82.0	61.6	71.8	1.73		

TABLE VIII.—*Monthly meteorological data, March to August, 1908, Washington, D. C.—*
Continued.

JULY.

Date.	Temperature.			Precipitation.	Character of day.	Possible sunshine.
	Maximum.	Minimum.	Mean.			
	°F.	°F.	°F.	Inches.		Per cent.
1....	90	69	80	0.01	Partly cloudy	86
2....	90	72	81	.03	.....do	78
3....	86	71	78	Trace.	.....do	58
4....	88	73	80	.24	.....do	43
5....	86	71	78	Trace.	.....do	56
6....	94	72	83	.00	.....do	82
7....	94	72	83	.04	Clear	98
8....	81	64	72	.00	Partly cloudy	66
9....	80	59	70	.00	.....do	67
10....	79	60	70	.00	.....do	59
11....	90	61	76	.00	Clear	92
12....	99	68	84	.05	Partly cloudy	69
13....	96	70	83	.00	Clear	93
14....	96	74	85	.06	Partly cloudy	64
15....	87	71	79	.00	Clear	78
16....	81	62	72	.00	.....do	98
17....	87	57	72	.00	.....do	78
18....	91	72	82	Trace.	Partly cloudy	56
19....	91	76	84	.00	.....do	71
20....	90	71	80	.00	.....do	67
21....	88	69	78	.20	Cloudy	57
22....	87	70	78	.13	.....do	38
23....	89	71	80	.77	.....do	41
24....	88	69	78	.17	.....do	46
25....	88	70	79	.05	.....do	38
26....	81	71	76	.88	.....do	19
27....	78	68	73	.65	.....do	3
28....	84	68	76	.00	Partly cloudy	48
29....	85	66	76	Trace.	.....do	62
30....	84	68	76	.00	.....do	73
31....	80	72	76	.01	Cloudy	0
Mean or total..	87.4	68.6	78.0	3.29		

AUGUST.

1....	84	66	75	0.00	Partly cloudy	65
2....	89	59	74	.00	Clear	100
3....	92	66	79	.00	.....do	89
4....	95	70	82	.00	.....do	91
5....	89	72	80	.02	Cloudy	36
6....	85	71	78	.06	.....do	16
7....	87	69	78	.01	.....do	26
8....	78	65	72	Trace.	.....do	31
9....	70	62	66	.86	.....do	1
10....	84	60	72	.00	Clear	92
11....	86	68	77	.00	.....do	85
12....	92	65	78	.00	.....do	72
13....	93	73	83	.00	.....do	99
14....	93	72	82	.00	Partly cloudy	75
15....	88	74	81	.00	.....do	57
16....	84	68	76	Trace.	Cloudy	28
17....	87	68	78	1.11	.....do	18
18....	86	70	78	.18	Partly cloudy	38
19....	89	70	80	.00	Clear	68
20....	77	59	68	Trace.	Partly cloudy	61
21....	80	53	66	.00	.....do	74
22....	84	69	76	Trace.	Cloudy	20
23....	79	71	75	Trace.	.....do	15
24....	74	66	70	.00	.....do	5
25....	68	56	62	1.84	.....do	0
26....	61	57	59	1.05	.....do	0
27....	63	56	60	.01	.....do	0
28....	67	58	62	.00	.....do	6
29....	76	52	64	.00	Clear	89
30....	81	52	66	.00	.....do	98
31....	81	56	68	.00	.....do	100
Mean or total..	82.0	64.3	73.2	5.14		

TABLE IX. — *Comparison of monthly meteorological data for 1908 with the average for thirty-eight years.*

Month.	Temperature.			Rainfall.		
	Mean for 1908.	Mean for thirty-eight years.	Average daily excess or deficiency as compared with mean for thirty-eight years.	Total for 1908.	Mean for thirty-eight years.	Monthly excess or deficiency as compared with mean for thirty-eight years.
	° F.	° F.	° F.	Inches.	Inches.	Inches.
March......	47.4	42.3	+5.1	2.45	3.93	−1.48
April.......	56.5	53.0	+3.5	1.59	3.14	−1.55
May........	65.2	64.0	+1.2	6.10	3.81	+2.29
June.......	71.8	72.6	−0.8	1.73	4.08	−2.35
July........	78.0	77.0	+1.0	3.29	4.61	−1.32
August.....	73.2	74.6	−1.4	5.14	4.43	+0.71

SUMMARY FOR 1908.

The results on the apple trees were the same as in 1907, that is, the foliage was not injured in any case from applications of pure lead arsenate or any of the by-products naturally formed in its manufacture.

Rather severe injury was caused to the foliage and fruit of the peach by pure lead arsenate, made either from lead acetate or lead nitrate, and the same was true when the salts formed as by-products in the making were not washed out, whether applied with or without lime. The fruit was of a deep red color which generally extended throughout the flesh, and maturity was hastened about one week.

Lead nitrate caused severe injury to the foliage but not to the fruit. Lead acetate in the stronger application caused slight injury to the foliage, but very materially protected the fruit from insect injury. Sodium acetate and acetic acid, acetic acid alone, and sodium nitrate produced no injurious effect on the foliage or fruit in the strengths applied.

The meteorological conditions from March to August, 1908, were very different from those for the same period in 1907. In general the temperature was considerably above the normal, and the rainfall was very much below normal except for May and August. One-half of the total rainfall for May (nearly as much as the normal average for the month) fell on two consecutive days. During June and most of July the rainfall was very light. No injury from previous spraying could be detected on May 25, when the final application was made. Five hot, clear days, without rain, followed this application, and on June 4, ten days after the application, very decided injury was observed. From the appearance of the foliage the injury would probably have been noticeable several days previously, but no observations had been made. This would seem to indicate very strongly that practically all the injury resulted from this last application.

SUMMARY OF RESULTS FOR THE TWO YEARS' EXPERIMENT.

No injury resulted to apple foliage in either 1907 or 1908 from three applications of lead arsenate, made from sodium arsenate and lead acetate, or sodium arsenate and lead nitrate, when applied at the rate of 1½ pounds (dry basis) to 50 gallons of water

No injury resulted to apple foliage in 1908 from the use of lead arsenate made by the two methods, from which the salts formed as by-products were not removed, when applied the same number of times and at the same rate   (This experiment was not tried in 1907.)

No injury was caused to the foliage of the apple in 1907 or 1908 by three applications of lead acetate or lead nitrate in strength greater than would occur in any but the most carelessly made lead arsenate

No injury was caused to the foliage of the apple in 1907 or 1908 from three applications of sodium acetate and acetic acid, acetic acid alone, or sodium nitrate,[a] in strengths produced from the amounts formed in the preparation of 1½ pounds of lead arsenate by the two methods, made to 50 gallons   These results were expected, as lead arsenate is being used in apple orchards very extensively in all parts of the country and with success

No noticeable injury resulted to peach foliage in 1907 from two or three applications of lead arsenate (made by the two methods) at the rate of 1½ pounds (dry basis) to 50 gallons of water   The fruit from these trees was a bright red color, which was desirable rather than otherwise, as its quality was not impaired.

Three applications of lead arsenate of the same strength (made by the two methods) in 1908 caused very marked injury to peach foliage and also to the fruit   The same when applied with lime in the proportion of 4 pounds to 50 gallons produced considerable injury, but to a less extent.   Injury to the fruit was decreased about 50 per cent by the use of lime.

In 1908 three applications of lead arsenate, made from sodium arsenate and lead acetate, and from sodium arsenate and lead nitrate, without removing the salts formed as by-products, resulted in the same injury as from the use of the washed product   The same applied with lime at the rate of 4 pounds to 50 gallons produced about 50 per cent less injury to the fruit.

Three applications of lead nitrate, in the proportion of 2 1 ounces and 4.2 ounces to 50 gallons of water, produced slight injury to peach

---

[a] Lodeman reports injury to the foliage of apple and quince from the application of nitrate of soda at the rate of 2 ounces in 2 gallons of water   Cornell Agr Exper Sta , 1893, Bul No 60, p 291

foliage in 1907 from the stronger application and very marked injury in 1908 from both strengths. No injurious effect on the fruit could be detected

Three applications of lead acetate at the rate of 2 7 ounces to 50 gallons of water produced no injurious effect on fruit or foliage in either 1907 or 1908.   Three applications of lead acetate at the rate of 5.4 ounces to 50 gallons produced no injurious effect in 1907 and slight injury to foliage in 1908   The use of the latter strength showed a very marked effect on the fruit in reducing the injury caused by insects   This material would probably prove very effective as an insecticide if applied frequently enough or if the applications were followed by a few days of dry weather.

No injury was caused to the foliage or fruit of the peach in 1907 or 1908 by three applications of sodium acetate and acetic acid, acetic acid alone, or sodium nitrate of the strengths in which they would occur in making 1½ pounds of lead arsenate without removing these products and making up to 50 gallons

As far as the protection of the fruit from insect injury is concerned, the lead arsenate was a success

GENERAL DISCUSSION OF PROBLEMS INVOLVED IN THE INVESTIGATION.

Naturally, the first question asked will be, Why did no injury result to the peach in 1907 from the application of lead arsenate, while in 1908, when the applications were made in the same way and of the same strength, serious injury resulted? Though our present knowledge is not sufficient to give a positive answer to this question, some very interesting results bearing on this point have been obtained.

LEAD NITRATE VS. LEAD ACETATE.

Contrary to the opinion held by many, lead arsenate made from sodium arsenate and lead nitrate did not cause any more injury than that made from sodium arsenate and lead acetate. Cases reported in which it has been more injurious may have been due to the presence of lead nitrate in considerable excess, for lead nitrate, as these experiments have shown, is considerably more caustic in its effect on foliage than lead acetate. Lead arsenate prepared from lead nitrate possesses several qualities which make it slightly more desirable for spraying purposes than that prepared from lead acetate. These have been pointed out in Part II.   It would be more dangerous to use, however, if not properly made—that is, if the lead nitrate were present in any considerable excess over that sufficient to combine with all the arsenic. The injury to the foliage caused by lead acetate appeared to be local in character, as it did not cause the leaves to fall

or turn yellow. In very minute quantities arsenic appears to exert
a stimulating effect or act as a tonic, as it does on animals. It is
probably this action which, by accelerating the functional activity
of the leaf and producing more rapid assimilation, causes the excess-
ive reddening and hastens the maturity of the fruit. On the other
hand, if too large an amount is absorbed, it has a toxic effect, resulting
in retarded assimilation, which in turn will cause the fruit to shrivel
and drop before it has matured

SUSCEPTIBILITY OF PEACH FOLIAGE TO INJURY.

It has not been satisfactorily explained why the stone fruits, the
peach in particular, should be so susceptible to injury Numerous
investigators have carried on extensive experiments on this point
with copper compounds, mostly Bordeaux mixture, and with Paris
green, resulting in much valuable information on the subject and the
advancement of several theories to account for it. Those who have
given special study to the action of fungicides and insecticides on
plants and foliage include numerous foreign investigators Among
those in this country the following may be mentioned: Gillette,[a]
Galloway,[b] Galloway and Woods, [c] Fairchild,[d] Sturgis, [e] Bain,[f] and
Hedrick [g]

It has been shown that leaves formed in a moist atmosphere have
a thinner and more easily permeable cuticle than those grown in a
dry atmosphere, and that injury from Bordeaux mixture and arsenicals is more severe in warm, damp weather. Gillette [h] says. "The
oldest leaves are most susceptible to injury," also, "foliage most
exposed to dew and direct sunlight will be most injured by the
arsenites, other things being equal. Leaves kept perfectly dry can
hardly be injured by the arsenites." Woodworth and Colby [i] "It
has been demonstrated repeatedly that dry Paris green can be placed
upon a leaf in any quantity and so long as the leaf remains dry no
evil results will follow "

No experiments have been made in this investigation with lead
arsenate to determine whether or not injury would result to peach
foliage in the absence of water. It was assumed that none would
be caused, in view of the results obtained by others with Paris green,

a Iowa Agr Exper Sta , 1890, Bul 10
b U S Dept Agr , Div Veg Path , 1892, Bul 3, 1894, Bul 7
c Proc Soc Prom Agr Sci , 1895, p 42
d U S Dept Agr , Div Veg Path , 1894, Bul 6
e Connecticut Agr Exper Sta , Ann Rep , 1900, Pt III, p 219
f Tennessee Agr Exper Sta , 1895, Vol 8, No 3, 1902, Vol 15, No 2
g New York Agr Exper Sta , 1907, Bul 287
h Iowa Agr Exper Sta , 1890, Bul 10, pp 402–403
i California Agr Exper Sta , 1899, Bul 126, pp 10–11.

which compound, under the usual conditions, is more injurious to foliage than lead arsenate.

Duggar[a] reports an extreme case in which bright sunshine following rain caused the appearance of "shot holes" in peach foliage. Others have also reported injury under these conditions, and it has been attributed to the concentration of the sun's rays on one spot by means of the drops of water acting as a lens and causing burning A disease of the peach, shown to be of bacterial origin, has also been reported,[b] which produces "shot holes" in the foliage and which is much worse in wet seasons.

The work here reported has shown that pure lead arsenate applied to tender foliage like the peach will, in some cases, cause serious injury, indicating, therefore, that there is some influencing condition not as yet satisfactorily determined which causes the material to be decomposed and the arsenic to go into solution This fact led to other experiments in the effort to discover the cause of this decomposition.

CAUSE OF THE DECOMPOSITION OF LEAD ARSENATE

EXPERIMENTS ON THE ACTION OF THE CARBON DIOXID OF THE AIR

The first idea that presented itself as a possible explanation for this decomposition of lead arsenate was that the carbon dioxid of the air might act on the lead arsenate, forming lead carbonate, and thus liberate the arsenic acid. This theory, however, did not seem to be very plausible from a chemical point of view and also owing to the lack of uniformity in the injury reported in different years and at different places, but it was decided to determine the point. In order to do so the following experiments were carried out

Experiment 1 —One gram of lead arsenate, made from sodium arsenate and lead acetate, was treated with 1,000 cc of cold distilled water which had been previously boiled to expel carbon dioxid This was allowed to stand ten days, being shaken eight times each day, and was then filtered At the end of ten days the amount of arsenic in the solution was determined

Experiment 2 —One gram of lead arsenate made from sodium arsenate and lead nitrate was treated in the same way

Experiment 3 —Same as Experiment 1, except that unboiled distilled water was used and carbon-dioxid gas was run into the solution for about one-half hour each day for ten days

Experiment 4 —Same as Experiment 3, except that lead arsenate was used as in Experiment 2

Experiment 5 —Same as Experiment 3, except that the solution was kept at about 50° C during the day

Experiment 6 —Same as Experiment 4, heating to 50° C each day (This is probably a higher temperature than the material would ever attain on the tree)

a New York Cornell Agr Exper Sta , 1899, Bul 164
b Ann. Rep. Conn Agr. Exper Sta , 1903, p 337, Mycologia, 1909, 1 23

TABLE X.—*Results of experiments with carbon dioxid.*

[Arsenic in solution expressed as As_2O_5.]

Carbon-dioxid-free water: .... *Per cent.*
　Experiment 1 .... 0. 40
　Experiment 2 49
Water with carbon dioxid added:
　Experiment 3 25
　Experiment 4 39
Water with carbon dioxid added and warmed to 50° C.:
　Experiment 5 33
　Experiment 6 43

It will be seen from these experiments that lead arsenate is slightly less soluble in distilled water saturated with carbon dioxid, even when heated to 50° C., than in cold distilled water free from carbon dioxid. It would hardly be expected that the results could be otherwise on the tree.

EXPERIMENTS ON THE SOLVENT ACTION OF WATER USED IN SPRAYING.

It was then thought that possibly the water with which the lead arsenate was being mixed for spraying contained compounds that had a solvent action on the lead arsenate. To determine this and also at the same time to determine the action of dilute solutions of sodium chlorid and sodium carbonate (two salts occurring frequently in waters) on lead arsenate, the following experiments were made:

Experiment 1.—One gram of lead arsenate, made from lead acetate, was treated with 1,000 cc of the water which was used in the spraying experiments, and allowed to stand at room temperature ten days, shaking it eight times each day. This was filtered and the amount of arsenic in the solution determined.

Experiment 2.—Same as Experiment 1, except that lead nitrate was used in making the lead arsenate.

Experiment 3.—Same as Experiment 1, except that the mixture was heated to about 50° C. each day for ten days.

Experiment 4.—Same as Experiment 2, except that the solution was heated as in Experiment 3.

Experiment 5.—Same as Experiment 1, except that the lead arsenate was treated with 1,000 cc of distilled water, carbon-dioxid-free, in which had been dissolved 2 grams of pure sodium chlorid.

Experiment 6.—Same as Experiment 5, using lead arsenate prepared from lead nitrate.

Experiment 7.—Same as Experiment 1, except that 1,000 cc of distilled water containing in solution 2 grams of pure sodium carbonate was used.

Experiment 8.—Same as Experiment 7, using lead arsenate prepared from lead nitrate.

The amount of arsenic in solution and the per cent based on the total arsenic present are given in the following table:

TABLE XI.—*Results of experiments to determine solvent action of water constituents on lead arsenate.*

[Arsenic in solution expressed as As_2O_5.]

Kind of lead arsenate and water treatment used.	Arsenic in solution.	
	Per cent based on weight of lead arsenate taken.	Per cent of total arsenic present.
Water used in spraying experiments:	*Per cent.*	*Per cent.*
Used cold—		
Experiment 1 (lead arsenate made from lead acetate)	5.24	17.61
Experiment 2 (lead arsenate made from lead nitrate)	3.61	11.06
Heated to 50° C.—		
Experiment 3 (lead arsenate made from lead acetate)	8.42	28.29
Experiment 4 (lead arsenate made from lead nitrate)	8.27	25.34
Water containing 0.2 per cent of sodium chlorid:		
Experiment 5 (lead arsenate made from lead acetate)	9.20	30.91
Experiment 6 (lead arsenate made from lead nitrate)	11.22	34.38
Water containing 0.2 per cent of sodium carbonate:		
Experiment 7 (lead arsenate made from lead acetate)	9.56	32.12
Experiment 8 (lead arsenate made from lead nitrate)	11.82	36.21

It will be seen from these results that a very large amount of arsenic has been dissolved, not only by the solutions of the two salts tried, but by the sample of water tested. It would appear, therefore, that the frequent injury reported from the use of lead arsenate may be due to the solvent action of the water used in applying it. To elucidate this point the composition of the water that had been used in the spraying experiments reported herein was determined. The results are given in Table XII:

TABLE XII.—*Analysis of water used in spraying experiments.*

[Water Laboratory, Miscellaneous Division.]

Constituent.	Parts per million.	Grains per gallon.	Constituent.	Parts per million.	Grains per gallon.
Silica (SiO_2)	23.2	1.353	Magnesium (Mg)	4.3	0.251
Sulphuric-acid radicle (SO_4)	7.4	.432	Potassium (K)	1.0	.058
Bicarbonic-acid radicle (HCO_3)	37.5	2.187	Sodium (Na)	20.9	1.219
Nitric-acid radicle (NO_3)	13.5	.787	Oxygen (to form Fe_2O_3)	.2	.012
Chlorin (Cl)	20.5	1.195			
Iron and aluminum (Fe and Al)	.6	.035	Total	134.6	7.850
Calcium (Ca)	5.5	.321			

HYPOTHETICAL COMBINATIONS

	Parts per million.	Grains per gallon.		Parts per million.	Grains per gallon.
Potassium chlorid (KCl)	1.9	0.111	Calcium bicarbonate ($CaHCO_3$)	22.3	1.301
Sodium chlorid (NaCl)	32.3	1.884	Ferric oxid (Fe_2O_3)	.8	.047
Sodium nitrate ($NaNO_3$)	18.5	1.079	Silica (SiO_2)	23.2	1.353
Sodium sulphate (Na_2SO_4)	9.9	.577			
Magnesium sulphate ($MgSO_4$)	.9	.052	Total	134.6	7.850
Magnesium bicarbonate ($MgHCO_3$)	24.8	1.446			

While the total amount of dissolved salts occurring in this water is small, it will be noticed that the sodium chlorid content is relatively high, and to this the solvent action which this water exerts on lead arsenate is no doubt largely due. It would appear from these results that if certain salts commonly occurring in waters are present in more than very small amounts they will exert a solvent action on the lead arsenate.

CONCLUSIONS.

Referring again to the fact that no injury resulted in 1907 from the lead arsenate, while in 1908 severe damage followed the use of the same water and chemicals, this may be explained by the difference between the two seasons with respect to climatic conditions. In 1907 every application was followed by cool, cloudy weather and rain within forty-eight hours. In 1908 the first two applications were followed by cool days and light rains soon thereafter, but the last application, which caused practically all of the injury, was followed by five clear, hot days and no rain. The dews at night would be sufficient to moisten the material, and when hot sunshine followed the conditions would be just right to dissolve the maximum amount of arsenic, and therefore cause the maximum injury. The salts (sodium chlorid and sodium carbonate and no doubt others which have not been tried), which cause the lead arsenate to be broken up, are readily soluble in water, and if their application were followed by rain they would be washed out, and therefore no injury should result.

Headden,[a] in a publication which has recently been issued, calls attention to the danger that may result from using water containing certain salts. He says: "It has often been asked at meetings of these orchardists whether it was a safe practice to use their surface alkali water in applying the lead arsenate and I have stated that it was not a good practice, for one could easily conceive of conditions under which the whole of the lead arsenate could be converted into sulphate of lead and sodic arsenate be formed in solution. This statement never seemed to be an acceptable one. I have in this case not depended upon any chemical laws, however evident their adequacy might be, but took well-washed lead arsenate, a sample which we found by rigid test to be free from soluble arsenic, suspended 1 gram of it in 2,000 times its weight of water and added 2 grams of Glauber's salt, allowed it to stand three days, filtered off a portion of it, concentrated by evaporation, and tested it for arsenic. I found

---

[a] Colorado Agr Exper Sta, 1908, Bul 131, p 22.

that the arsenic had gone into solution in very considerable quantities A parallel experiment was carried out with salt, in which only 1 gram of salt was used to the 2,000 grams of water This was not allowed to stand quite three days when 1,500 grams were filtered off, concentrated and tested for arsenic This concentrated solution was found to be so heavily charged with arsenic that only a small part of it gave an unmanageable amount of arsenic when brought into an active Marsh apparatus "

Still more exhaustive experiments than those here reported are being made in the orchard this year, which it is hoped will definitely settle this point It was deemed best to report the progress that has been made before waiting for the final conclusions or for the results of other experiments along the same line, some of which have suggested themselves since this work was begun The full data obtained from the 1909 experiments have not as yet been collated, but some interesting results have been obtained and may be briefly mentioned Lead arsenate was applied to peach trees in the same proportions as in previous experiments—that is, 1½ pounds (dry basis) to 50 gallons—and three applications were made

(1) When applied with spring water (analysis of which has been given), some injury to foilage resulted, but it was not nearly so marked as in the preceding year, and a longer time elapsed before the injury was noticeable

(2) When applied with distilled water very slight injury occurred, noticeably less than when the spring water was used

(3) When applied with distilled water to which 10 grains per gallon of sodium chlorid had been added, rather serious injury resulted When distilled water containing 40 grains of sodium chlorid per gallon was used, the injury was very much increased, practically 50 per cent of the foilage being affected.

(4) When applied with distilled water containing 10 grains of sodium carbonate per gallon, injury was noticeable fourteen days after the first application, and seven days after the third application the trees were almost completely defoliated

(5) Applied with distilled water containing 10 and 40 grains of sodium sulphate per gallon, some injury resulted, but this was not so marked as that produced in the presence of sodium chlorid

In similar experiments where lime was added at the rate of 4 pounds to 50 gallons, injury to the foilage was almost entirely prevented.

LIST OF TABLES.

O

Lightning Source UK Ltd.
Milton Keynes UK
UKHW020805250521
384341UK00006B/489